The Black Girl's Guide to Emotional Healing Devotional

Nijiama Smalls

ISBN- 978-1-7346928-3-9

To my husband Shamon who loves me without conditions. To my children Bliss and Jace: may you continue to pass down the legacy of emotional healing through the generations. To Pastor John K. Jenkins and First Lady Trina Jenkins. My life changed completely under your ministry, and for that, I will always be forever grateful.

To all my fellow Black girls that struggle just like I do, that have suffered from life's hurts as I have, may God give us the grace and power to grow, learn, heal, and build a sisterhood that empowers future generations.

Contents

Introduction

Sis,

I'm so delighted that you have decided to continue, or if you're new, thank you for starting, this healing journey with me. I know this is not easy, but hopefully you have discovered that it is well worth it. Removing the inner chaos from our lives and gaining peace is priceless.

Hopefully, you have already begun this journey by reading *The Black Girl's Guide to Healing Emotional Wounds*, which should be your first step, but it's good if you're starting here – it's all about getting healing from unhealed wounds. Now that you have taken steps to understand your need for healing, it's time to take a deeper look at who you are and the toxic thoughts and behaviors that you have embraced. It's also time to evaluate your self-love so that you can understand the areas that need to be mended to build your confidence.

As black girls, we have so much to conquer internally, and when we do so, that will help us reflect proper actions or behaviors externally. The constant thoughts that run through our minds daily can be overwhelming:

"Am I too thick?"

"Am I too thin?"

"Am I smart enough?"

"Am I pretty enough?"

"Am I loved?"

"Do I appear too desperate for love?"

"Am I too aggressive?"

"Did I overreact?"

"Why can't I make and maintain solid girlfriends?"

"Why can't I find a good man?"

The list goes on and on. This constant questioning of self that chips away at our self-esteem is typically caused by unhealed emotional wounds. If we do not heal the wounds, we will view the world and make important life decisions out of those hurts. When we overreact, make purchases to impress others, cut off friends too quickly, "clap back" at our supervisor, or lash out, we are acting out on unhealed wounds.

Studies have found that it takes between twenty-two and sixty days to establish new habits. In this book of devotions, day by day we will tackle our thoughts and feelings for thirty-seven days while unlearning toxic behaviors and replacing them with positive coping skills.[11] We are going to deal with the hurts that life has dealt us and assign new meanings to them.

I want to encourage you to make some alone time and find a quiet place to read this daily devotional, whether it is morning or night. Make this a part of your self-care routine because healing your wounds is the ultimate act of self-love and care. Complete the answers at the end of each devotional. These questions will allow you to reflect and will sharpen your awareness of self, as you cannot heal what you are unaware of. Complete the action items as it will help you put the principles into practice.

Each daily devotional begins with a passage of scripture. Scripture is powerful in that it stirs emotions, helps to change perspective, and build confidence. Trust me when I tell you that there is no other resource on this planet quite like it. Read the passage of scripture, memorize it, meditate on it, chew on it, digest it, and get it into your soul and spirit.

Please understand that this journey is completely about healing you – no one is judging or condemning you. Not even God. I'm certainly not judging you as I am still working out my own issues. Trust! But I am proud of you for doing this for yourself. It's one of the best gifts you will ever give yourself.

Also, you need to understand that this road is lonely at times. You will soon discover that not everyone is as interested in healing as you are and that alone can feel isolating. As you begin to see things from a different lens, you may begin to feel that some of the previous relationships you once had no longer are helpful for your next. Negative people will have a sheer disdain for you. Don't worry, God will send the right people along your path to love and care for you in a healthy way. Embrace these new relationships as they are now your emotional support system.

Sis, please know you are not alone; I am on this journey with you – I've had my share of inner chaos to clean up. I'm honored that I get to hold your hand as we take these next steps in this journey.

So, let's begin…

Day 1

A Nasty Woman

Hebrews 11:31
By faith the harlot Rahab did not perish with those who did not believe, when she had received the spies with peace. [1]

Can I tell y'all that I just love me some Rahab? If Rahab was alive today, I'd hope she and I would be friends. I picture us meeting for brunch on Saturdays at trendy restaurants in downtown DC sipping mimosas as we engage in hours of girl chat.

During Biblical times, Rahab was referred to as a harlot, a sex worker, and a prostitute. In those days, prostitution was considered to be a very shameful act and many women were put to death by fire for it. Yikes! But my good sis Rahab did not allow this to stop her from believing in God and making history.

The Israelite Army sent spies to gather intel on the land in which Rahab lived before pursuing it. Rahab allowed the spies to spend the night in her home and hid them from the authorities. Check out Rahab's conversation with the spies:

Joshua 2:8-14: Now before they lay down, she came up to them on the roof, and said to the men: "I know that the LORD has given you the land, that the terror of you has fallen on us, and that all the inhabitants of the land are fainthearted because of you. For we have heard how the LORD dried up the water of the Red Sea for you when you came out of Egypt, and what you did to the two kings of the Amorites who were on the other side of the Jordan, Sihon and Og, whom you utterly destroyed. And as soon as we heard these things, our hearts melted; neither did there remain any more courage in anyone because of you, for the LORD your

God, He is God in heaven above and on earth beneath. Now therefore, I beg you, swear to me by the LORD, since I have shown you kindness, that you also will show kindness to my father's house, and give me a true token, and spare my father, my mother, my brothers, my sisters, and all that they have, and deliver our lives from death."

So the men answered her, "Our lives for yours, if none of you tell this business of ours. And it shall be, when the LORD has given us the land, that we will deal kindly and truly with you."[1]

Rahab had heard about God and had enough faith in Him that she knew He would deliver the land, the very one she lived in, into the hands of the Israelites. Like a boss, she stood boldly in front of them and negotiated with them. She did not allow shame, embarrassment, nor her socioeconomic status to make her feel inferior or stop her from asking for what she wanted.

Not only did the spies honor Rahab's wishes sparing her family's life, but she is the lineage that Jesus Christ was born into. Now I'm sure that God could have chosen any other family for Christ to be born into, perhaps one that was pure and had more prestige and innocence attached to them. But He didn't choose them. He chose Rahab — the prostitute. This proves to the world that her worth is valuable.

Sis, my prayer is that as you are reading these words you realize that you are not defined by your worst moments and there is nothing you have done or what people have deemed you to be that can stop you from living an amazing life filled with purpose. Release shame, condemnation, and judgments that you have about yourself. It does not matter what anyone else thinks of you. All that matters is what God says about you. Stand tall understanding who you are and that you are valuable. You have worth! You are enough!

Questions to Journal

What has caused you to feel shame?

_____
_____
_____
_____
_____
_____
_____
_____

What situations (past or present) cause you to feel judged?

_____
_____
_____
_____
_____
_____
_____
_____

What are some things that you typically judge yourself for (i.e., career, appearance, relationships, parenting, etc.)?

_____
_____
_____
_____
_____

Sis, Are you Bitter?

Hebrews 12:14-15
Pursue peace with all people, and holiness, without which no one will see the Lord: looking carefully lest anyone fall short of the grace of God; lest any root of bitterness springing up cause trouble, and by this many become defiled. [1]

Have you ever met a woman that has unresolved conflict with almost everyone in her life? She has conflict with her supervisor and colleagues at work. She has conflict with girlfriends and struggles to maintain long-term friendships. She has conflict with her parents and family members. She argues and fights with her lovers. She even argues with her ex-partner's new significant other. Perhaps this woman is you. This behavior is the sign of a bitter woman.

Bitterness is typically caused by some form of unhealed wound that was left untreated. When you do not heal, the wound remains open and it grows, manifesting into your subconscious, and bitterness forms. And, just like a mosquito bite when it's touched, every time someone does something that annoys you, the wound when poked is painfully activated. As the scripture says, "bitterness springs forth and causes trouble" and that can continue in effect for the rest of your life sabotaging your relationships and clouding your perspective.

I have experienced seasons in my life where I have been bitter and it was mainly because I was unhappy with where I was in life. I constantly focused on all the things that I did not have and all the wrong that other people did to me. During those times, I saw the negative in everything. Even in the most innocent of situations, I would find something negative about it to discuss. Then, I used harsh criticism as my weapon because for me, making someone else feel bad made me feel good, or so I thought. I had to get to the root of the issue and address my hurts to heal them because they were impacting my relationships and decisions.

It's also possible to have bitterness towards a specific person. When we focus heavily on the negative things that they do, become hyper critical of their actions, and overreact to their minor annoyances that's when we know we are harboring some bitterness towards them. Often, this is caused by holding on to something they did in the past that we have not let go of and it's controlling our relationship with them.

It is for this reason that God encourages us to pursue peace. "Pursue" is a verb, which means peace requires action on our part. We should be swift to apologize when we are wrong and open to reconciling to prevent bitterness from forming, always extending forgiveness. Reconciliation does not mean we do not maintain healthy boundaries, but it simply means we have forgiven and made peace with the person and the situation.

Are you bitter? If so, it's time to heal.

Questions to Journal

Which emotions do you need to release or transform
(i.e., bitterness, anger, inferiority, selfishness, shame)?

_____

_____

_____

_____

_____

_____

_____

_____

How have these emotions impacted your
relationships?

_____

_____

_____

_____

_____

_____

_____

Day 3

Childish Things

1 Corinthians 13:11
When I was a child, I spoke as a child, I understood as a
child, I thought as a child; but when I became a man, I put
away childish things. [1]

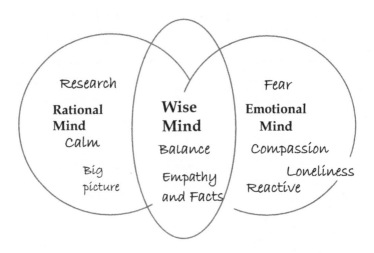

My son is five years old. When we tell him to go to bed, he lashes out, screams, slams the door, calls us names, such as poopy head and meanie, and tosses his pillows, sheet, and blanket onto the floor. We give him a few minutes to give us the silent treatment, then we return to his room. By that time, we find him cuddled comfortably in his bed, clutching his blanket with his thumb or finger in his mouth fast asleep. There are adults that exhibit the same behavior when they are told things they do not want to hear.

The largest indicator of unhealed emotional wounds is our reactions. The way in which you react, overreact, or act out, when things do not go your way, or someone offends you show if you are thriving emotionally.

When you are emotionally mature, you realize that the power is in using your wise mind (the intersection of the logical and emotional mind) to make decisions and to resolve conflict.[4] Often we tend to use the emotional part of our brain to make decisions and that causes us to make harmful decisions that wreak havoc and burn bridges. For example, if a friend tells you that another friend hurt her and you rely solely on empathy and compassion for your friend, it may cause you to take the side of your friend and unfriend the other friend without hearing the other side. That could result in the loss of a quality friendship.

I've found that the person that has mastered calmness and remains logical during conflict is the one that passes the test. It requires a certain level of control of self and maturity to remain calm and logical during a heated conversation or difficult moment. It also means that you are using the rational thinking part of your brain, the part that knows the true reality. Of course, you are going to experience emotions during conflict such as fear and anger and that is perfectly okay, but tuning into your wise mind adds a balance and will help those feelings to remain at bay allowing you to think logically.

I once watched a neighbor (a well-educated professional in her thirties) yell, kick, scream, curse, name call, and threaten to harm someone during a minor disagreement. She used the emotional part of her mind. Additionally, behaving irrationally in a disagreement is also an indicator of unhealed trauma. When severe trauma occurs early in our development, our emotional maturity tends to stop at the age the trauma occurred. This is also behavior displayed when we pursue addictive behaviors (i.e., heavy drinking, taking illegal narcotics, or promiscuity) in our early development. These situations stunt our emotions, and we will remain stuck in an arrested development not matching the maturity of our peers in our age demographic until we pursue healing.

As you are on your journey, please include mindfulness mediation. This is an easy technique that teaches you to control your actions by controlling your thoughts. Secondly, seeing a therapist is essential. A therapist can not only be your sounding board, but provide you the tools and techniques to further manage your emotions.

Questions to Journal

Which of the three minds do you typically rely on to resolve conflict and handle tough situations?

_____

_____

_____

_____

_____

_____

_____

What has been the result?

_____

_____

_____

_____

_____

_____

Day 4

The Battle Is All In Your Mind

Proverbs 23:7
For as he thinks in his heart, so is he.[1]

It was found that the average person has around 30,000 thoughts per day. Of those thousands of thoughts, 80% were negative, and 95% were exactly the same repetitive thoughts as the day before.[7]

Our thoughts impact our beliefs and emotions and our beliefs and emotions impact our actions. The greatest power that we have comes in the form of our thoughts. Our thought life determines our truth and reality. And often that is where most of our inner chaos stems.

My husband and his sister were both traumatized by events that happened during their childhood. They experienced the same trauma, but because of their thought patterns, they interpreted the trauma differently thus experiencing vastly different life outcomes. It's not always the trauma that impacts us, but the stories we tell ourselves about the trauma that has the largest impact on our lives.

We have to learn to take inventory of our thoughts so that we can begin to change the narrative in our heads. For example, if you were abused, instead of thinking that you were a victim of abuse, begin to view it as you survived abuse. Honey, let me tell you there is power in viewing yourself as a survivor and an overcomer! This simple shift can be a real game changer in your life.

As another example, if your mother was not present to parent you when you were a child, please know that God may have removed her for a reason. Perhaps God had special plans for you and that required you to be parented differently.

For a final example, if your mother parented poorly, it is quite possible that you, as a parent, understand how important your role and presence is in your child's life so you parent far differently than you were parented. In a nutshell, your mother's lack of positive parenting made you a better parent.

Whatever awful things that you may have had to overcome, please know that you now have a story to tell and that story has the power to impact others. I have found that the most profound individuals on this planet are the ones that have a messy past because they have a story to tell. They also have gained wisdom and insight from their hurts and mistakes.

We also need to check our thoughts to see if they include blame. Like a flame to a torch, blame fuels anger and will even cause us to lash out. When we make statements of blame such as "it's all her fault" or "my life would have been better if it wasn't for xyz," we are giving our power to other people instead of owning the decisions we made that control our lives. This is a victim mentality that will keep you constantly searching for sympathy and feeling inferior. It will also prevent you from healing because blame is the antithesis of self-awareness.

Let's take inventory of our thoughts and kick out the ones that cause us harm.

Questions to Journal

What negative thoughts tend to plague you the most?

_____

_____

_____

_____

_____

_____

_____

_____

Action Item

Over the next few days, practice kicking out of your mind the negative thoughts that do not serve you.

_____
_____
_____
_____
_____
_____
_____
_____
_____
_____
_____
_____
_____

Day 5

Take Off the Limits

Joshua 1:9
Have I not commanded you? Be strong and courageous. Do
not be afraid; do not be discouraged, for the Lord your God
will be with you wherever you go.[1]

"If you accept a limiting belief then it will become true for
you," Louise Hay.

"So, statistically, when a police officer sees a brown man like
my Jude walking down the road — as opposed to my white
nerdy kids walking down the road — because of the statistics
that he knows in his head, that these police officers know in
their head, they're going to know that statistically my brown
son is more likely to commit a violent offense over my white
sons.... The fact that in his head, he would be more careful
around my brown son than my white son, that doesn't
actually make me angry. That makes that police officer
smart, because of statistics." These are the words that were
spoken by Abby Johnson (a white woman and conservative
activist) regarding her adopted biracial son. [5] This is a prime
example of self-limiting beliefs. These are beliefs that over
time we have not only accepted but fully embraced. They are
not helpful at all as they hinder and cripple us. They prevent
us from seeing the new opportunities that are present for us
with each day. And often, we do not get the results we want
because of our lack of action controlled by our limiting
beliefs.

It bothers me tremendously that Abby Johnson made these comments about her son. As his mother, her role is to build his set of beliefs and train of thought that will ultimately impact his actions. I, personally, know many black men that have overcome the statistics, including my husband.

Born and raised in the heart of Washington DC, in a crime infested neighborhood, my husband's parents divorced and his mother abandoned him as a teenager due to mental illness, leaving him to be raised by a neighbor. Obviously, the odds were stacked against him. Today my husband, who graduated summa cum laude from high school, has earned a MS degree, is a Pastor of a church, and a leader of a defense program that employs hundreds of people. He is an amazing, self-aware, and self-controlled husband, father, and god-father. He has never committed a crime and is quite possibly the kindest human you will ever meet, often referred to as the "gentle giant" by those that know him well. Perhaps he accomplished all of this because of his self-will and determination, or perhaps it is because he had someone in his life that believed in him so much that they never allowed him to be defined by statistics and self-limiting beliefs. Had he bought in to these types of limiting beliefs, he may have made a completely different set of choices.

Do any of these limiting beliefs sound familiar to you?
- I need love and approval from those significant to me.
- I'm too old.
- I'm not smart enough.
- I am not worthy.
- I'm not educated enough.
- I'm afraid of trying and failing.
- I'm not pretty enough.
- I do not speak well enough.

- I never have anything insightful to add to a conversation.
- I am too bad.
- I've made too many mistakes in my past.
- I'm not in his league.
- I don't feel that I deserve it.
- All men are dogs.
- All black boys are doomed to a lifetime of trouble.
- I'm afraid to fail because failure is bad.

These are the beliefs that dwell inside of our minds and subconsciously, they prevent us from doing all of the things we need to do.

Some of these beliefs come from our caregivers. My mom and aunts used to say "all men are dogs." So I believed that and that's what I attracted in my early dating experiences. My grandfather, who grew up during the great depression, used to say "money is scarce." So he behaved as such regardless of how much he had always holding on tightly to every dime he earned out of fear of scarcity.

Please know that these beliefs are contrary to everything God has planned for us. The Bible, in Philippians 4:13 says, "I can do all things through Christ that strengthens me." Do you remember this from attending Sunday school as a kid? lol. Our Creator does not want us to be controlled by beliefs that limit us because they are counterproductive and hold us back.

We have to identify and destroy these beliefs that interfere with our progress. Not only do we need to uproot and destroy them but replace them with beliefs that empower us. Nothing should have the ability to hold us back from living our dreams or having an abundant life filled with joy, peace, and hope.

Questions to Journal

Identify any limiting beliefs that may be holding you
back in the space below.

_____

_____

_____

_____

_____

_____

_____

Where does each limiting belief come from?

_____

_____

_____

_____

_____

_____

_____

Action Item

Consider ways that you can reframe your limiting ideas. Journal about a limiting idea and a new way to reframe that limiting thought.

For example, if you believe that all black men are doomed to a life of failure then reframe the thought to something such as: "There are many black men that are thriving and successful and my son/husband/family members will be one of them."

_____

_____

_____

_____

_____

_____

_____

_____

_____

_____

_____

_____

God Will Test Your Gangsta' in the Workplace

Proverbs 21:1
The king's heart is in the hand of the LORD,
Like the rivers of water;
He turns it wherever He wishes.[1]

I've been a leader for quite some time. I've seen many people that genuinely desire upward mobility. They crave the title, Manager, Supervisor, Director, or Vice President, and the earnings increase that is attached to it, but do not understand how to obtain it. I've watched as subordinates act-the-fool when things do not go their way. I've seen employees curse out their manager, gossip about them behind their back, and completely disregard instructions given to them, but yet they are offended when they do not get the promotion or raise. But here's what I know: if you can't control your emotions as an employee, you can't control them as a leader, if you can't handle change as an employee, you can't handle it as a leader, if you can't follow directions as an employee, you won't follow them as a leader.

God has always tested my gangsta' in the workplace. I used to think I could "clap back" at my bosses because I could get away with it. I would also brag and boast about it to my friends and colleagues. I learned, the hard way, that there are consequences for bad behavior. My emotional immaturity was clouding my judgement. Therefore, my leaders could not see the potential inside of me because my toxic behavior was shielding it. I had to become emotionally mature before I was able to gain a promotion or title. I had to heal my wounds so that I would not take things personally and learn self-control so that I would not overreact when I was hurt or felt I was wronged.

As the scripture says, "the heart of the king is truly in God's hands". In modern terms, the king represents those in positions of power over us such as our bosses and leaders. Their actions, attitude, and behaviors towards us is often allowed by God because He is using them to change something inside of us. It's not always about our boss, but about God shaping and molding us to be better people. If you have a leader that you do not work well with, remove your focus from them and ask God what is it that He wants you to change about yourself.

Questions to Journal

If I were to contact your present and past managers, what would they say about your attitude and behavior at work?

_____
_____
_____
_____
_____
_____
_____

Has your attitude or behavior ever held you back from achieving your professional goals?

_____
_____
_____
_____
_____
_____
_____

Day 7

Black Girl Beauty!

Psalm 139:14-16
I will praise You, for I am fearfully and wonderfully made;
Marvelous are Your works,
And that my soul knows very well.
My frame was not hidden from You,
When I was made in secret,
And skillfully wrought in the lowest parts of the earth.
Your eyes saw my substance, being yet unformed.
And in Your book they all were written,
The days fashioned for me,
When as yet there were none of them.[1]

Can you imagine that there was a time in this country that what was considered mainstream beauty only included straight haired, blonde, or brunette women with blue or green eyes? The American edition of Vogue did not feature a black woman until 1974, roughly ten years after the British edition featured their first black American model. The first black woman to win Miss America, Vanessa Williams, was crowned in 1984. For many years, women such as Marilyn Monroe, Raquel Welch, Jan Shrimpton, and Twiggy were idolized for their beauty all because someone in a powerful position believed this is how beauty was to be symbolized. The rest of the country followed suit in that thought.

This sent black women a cruel message that still haunts us today; black women do not fit their subjective view of beauty. Why? I suppose because our looks are different. Perhaps they felt our skin was too dark, our noises were too large, our hips were too wide, and our hair was too kinky. As a community, we have internalized this message and it has left us with insecurities -generational insecurities. You see, many of our ancestors struggled to see themselves as beautiful because of our country's very toxic and limited view of beauty. Therefore, we inherited generational insecurities that I truly believe we still carry with us today. This is the reason that we question our beauty and compare ourselves to other women. These generational insecurities also cause us to put a lot of emphasis on our personal appearances and being "on point" at all times. It's the validation we are craving and this need for validation is also the thing that causes us to constantly check the social media selfies that we posted for likes, to see how many people truly find us beautiful. It also causes us to jump into the arms of the first man that adores our beauty.

When we have a disagreement with another woman, we are quick to put them down; "she's not pretty," "her hair is always a mess," "her nose is too big," "she's black and ugly," "she's so thick." We attack women in the very areas that we, as black women, are the most vulnerable. These are our generational unhealed emotional wounds speaking because wounded people wound people.

Today, although the definition of beauty has been widened to include black women, many of the images of black women in the media currently are exclusive to only a specific type of black woman, which is one with a European mix. In addition to this, many of us feel the sting of betrayal from our brothers because for many of them, once they gain global success, they abandon the traditional black woman for the ones that are closer to a European mix. Please understand that many of our brothers are suffering from unhealed generational wounds as well. They are striving for acceptance and approval in an environment that was not created for them. Because of this, they may select a partner that has been deemed beautiful by those in power. For them, it signifies they have arrived, they are now accepted, and can now have what they once couldn't afford.

Sis, you are beautiful! But there is a difference in knowing you are beautiful and feeling beautiful. I can tell you how beautiful you are all day every day, but if you don't feel it, then my words mean nothing. And feeling beautiful impacts your self-confidence.

I'm here to tell you that it does not matter if we do not meet anyone else's standard of beauty, God created you and me both as we are and there is nothing wrong with that. We are not cursed, we are not inferior, and we certainly are not gross. We have to recognize that our beauty and uniqueness is a living being of its own. We must appreciate the melanin in our skin that glows when we enter a room and contrasts so nicely against all the colors making us look amazing in almost any color that we wear. We must appreciate the cheek bone structure that adds variety to our face and our full lips that many would kill to have. Our diversity makes us special and our uniqueness brings something different to the spaces we enter. And because our history is complex, we carry an in-depth level of insight and wisdom.

We need to celebrate ourselves and each other and know that our blackness is a gift all on its own. Black women: we are ethereal, we are gorgeous, we are audacious, and more importantly we are blessed.

Questions to Journal

Do you feel beautiful?

_____
_____
_____
_____
_____
_____
_____
_____

If no, why not?

_____
_____
_____
_____
_____
_____
_____
_____

What makes you feel beautiful?

_____
_____
_____
_____
_____
_____
_____
_____

Action Item

If you struggle to believe that you are beautiful, stand in the mirror and compliment yourself. Try not to focus on what you don't like. Do this activity every morning focusing on a different area of your body as you are getting dressed.

Day 8

What Determines Your Value?

Isaiah 43:4
*Since you were precious in my sight, you have been honored,
and I have loved you;
Therefore I will give men for you, and people for your life.*[1]

A few years ago, I worked with a woman at an organization
in downtown DC where we were both leaders. She was a
sharp lady who came with a wealth of knowledge and
experiences. She was also rather ruthless. Anyone that she
perceived to be a threat, she would annihilate. She would
become defensive and overreact at the mere thought of
someone questioning her or her work. She was unforgiving
and quick to despise someone that didn't agree with her,
offered criticism, and did not fully submit to her will. She
spent lots of time fighting, delegating to gain power, arguing,
and trying to prove her points. What was created from her
behavior and leadership style was a team of disgruntled and
bitter employees. This is the behavior we display when our
worth and identity is found in positions and titles and not in
God.

We live in a society where the personal identity of many is based on superficial things. People will quickly tell you who they work for, what they do for a living, how much they earn, how large their house is, and the type of car they drive as soon as they meet you. This is the behavior of those that do not feel that their energy, personality, or principles will win you over, so they look to superficial things to do the job. This is also the behavior of those that have a neglected inner child that needs to be seen.

As the scripture says, we are precious in God's eyes. When we fully understand that we are valuable to God, we don't need to concern ourselves with impressing others, competing, or becoming angry when someone questions or disagrees with us. We know there is nothing that anyone can take from us if God has not allowed it to be taken. And if He allows anything to be taken away, then trust me when I tell you, there is something better on the horizon.

Ladies, can I be honest with y'all and tell you that there are days when I just do not feel that I am enough? Regardless of how many degrees I've earned, goals I have accomplished, and material possessions I've accumulated, I still question my worth. Here is what I had to realize; we are spiritual beings therefore earthly things and accomplishments were never meant to define or fulfill us; that's not their job. The pleasure derived from earthly possessions or accomplishments is temporal. We must focus on developing a relationship with our Creator and focusing on what He says about us. That's truly all that matters. As you focus on what God says, you will realize that all other things and opinions simply do not matter. These earthly things should not define us. A title, position, or status should not make or break us.

Questions to Journal

Describe who you are without using any of your titles.

_____

_____

_____

_____

_____

_____

_____

_____

It's Not Supposed to be this Way

I Kings 17:1-9

And Elijah the Tishbite, of the inhabitants of Gilead, said to Ahab, "As the LORD God of Israel lives, before whom I stand, there shall not be dew nor rain these years, except at my word."

Then the word of the LORD came to him, saying, "Get away from here and turn eastward, and hide by the Brook Cherith, which flows into the Jordan. And it will be that you shall drink from the brook, and I have commanded the ravens to feed you there."

So he went and did according to the word of the LORD, for he went and stayed by the Brook Cherith, which flows into the Jordan. The ravens brought him bread and meat in the morning, and bread and meat in the evening; and he drank from the brook. 7 And it happened after a while that the brook dried up, because there had been no rain in the land.

Then the word of the LORD came to him, saying, "Arise, go to Zarephath, which belongs to Sidon, and dwell there. See, I have commanded a widow there to provide for you."[1]

For the past few years, I had been working at what I would refer to as my dream job. It was for a great company that respected diversity and provided me with lots of opportunities. I was leading teams across the globe, traveling across the world, making decisions that impacted multitudes while earning a six-figure salary. I was the bomb.com! Suddenly, the talk of layoffs began as business needs began to shift and workloads became reduced. I survived several rounds of layoffs, but I could tell that the work continued to dry up. Inevitably, I too was laid off. Initially, it didn't bother me because I've never had issues finding work and as I anticipated, the interviews began to roll in. I bought a fresh interview suit and put my best foot forward wowing all of the interviewers and utilizing my connections.

Suddenly, the coronavirus became a global pandemic causing businesses to reorganize. The companies that I had great interviews with sent me communications stating they were now on a hiring freeze or beginning their own lay off process. Suddenly, my prospects began to dry up; the phone stopped ringing and no one was sending me emails. I did not expect this turn of events at all.

I grew frustrated. I was upset, frankly because the six-figure salary was gone. It was a blow to my ego as I also found myself asking, "Okay God, now what do I do?" I'm the kind of person that carefully plans everything to a tee and I like to be in control, so this totally threw me off. We had plans to travel out of the country with our family and to have some major additions made to our home. My kids were also involved in a multitude of summer activities and programs, which cost a lot of money. I knew things would have to change if I wasn't working full time. Not knowing what was next made me feel helpless. I prayed, "God, have you forgotten me?"

In my quiet time, I began to reflect on the year that I made the move to the Washington DC area. I was in my very early twenties, a recent college grad leaving my family, friends, and everything I knew behind. As time grew closer to moving, I became a bit apprehensive about the move. However, as I began to apply for jobs near my home town, I received rejection after rejection. That let me know it was time to relocate.

As a graduation gift, my grandmother provided me with a large sum of money, so I had enough to take care of my needs while I settled into the DC area. I had a family member that lived here that allowed me to live with her as I settled in. So, I hopped on Amtrak and made the one-way trip to Union Station. Little did I know, that a few years later, the DC area would be where I found God and learned what faith truly is. It would be the place that I developed my career and even acquired a master's degree. I met life-long friends that are now like family. The icing on the cake - I met and married my husband and now, 14 years and two kids later, the DC area is home for us. Through all of that, I learned that God is the maker and creator of the universe, so He certainly knows what is the best direction for our lives even when we don't see it.

So, during the time that I was laid off, I had a chance to focus on writing books, and helping my fellow sisters to heal. I was asked to participate in many virtual conferences, interviews, and wrote for various publications. Also, during this time, my husband received two major promotions that both came with rather hefty financial increases and the renters that are living in our rental property decided to renew their lease. I also had a part-time consulting job that got busier.

I've realized that God closes doors to confer direction. Just as He did for Elijah when the brook dried up, He uses circumstances to guide us and to tell us that He has something better planned for us. I can look back over my life and see how God removed friends that were no good for me, lovers that were toxic, and jobs that didn't always value me for something better. I can also see the doors that He opened - those were the doors that He meant for me to walk through. Those doors provided me with new friends that I have learned from and helped me to reach my goals. Through opened doors, God also provided a husband for me that has loved me more than anyone else on this planet and career positions that helped me to grow and increase my professional value. The list goes on and on. Believe me, I know it's hard to see it when we are in the midst of it. But we have to build up our trust to know that God has a plan for us and His plans are far better than our own.

Questions to Journal

Reflect on situations in your life where doors have been closed to you. Write one or a few of them down.

_____

_____

_____

_____

_____

_____

_____

_____

Using the previous situation(s) list what you have gained from those situations (i.e. new wisdom, new job, better partner etc.)?

_____

_____

_____

_____

_____

_____

_____

Day 10

Envious Decisions

Ephesians 5:20

Giving thanks always for all things to God the Father in the name of our Lord Jesus Christ.[1]

I once had a friend, Susan, who grew up in the inner city of DC. As a child, she experienced a challenging life as her parents fell victims to the crack cocaine epidemic. She attended a rather large church in DC as a teenager into her young adult years.

One Sunday, the pastor's daughter was driving a brand-new Lexus that her father had just purchased for her birthday. Susan watched her pastor's daughter, with head held high, drive the shiny, new car through the church parking lot barely acknowledging her. My friend was hurt by the pastor's daughter's behavior towards her. "One day, I'm going to buy a Lexus and I will show her how to drive it without having my nose stuck in the air," is what my friend thought to herself as she watched.

Several years later, Susan was an adult living in Prince George's County and busy raising her daughter. She had a great job and decided to upgrade her brand-new Honda Accord for a used Lexus. Little did she know when she grabbed the keys from the salesman and signed that check over to them, that Lexus was going to bring her lots of pain and regret. Girl, she had so much trouble with that car, from constant brake issues, the transmission malfunctioning, even the air bags deployed at the wrong time almost causing her physical harm. Her mechanic grew frustrated with her, "I told you not to buy this car!" She became angry with the time and money she had to put into repairing the car. At her wits end, she prayed to God, crying out to Him asking, "why is this happening to me? This is my dream car and I'm your child. Do I not deserve nice things? God, why is this car causing me so many problems?" God simply responded to her saying, "you bought this car out of envy of your pastor's daughter and not out of your own healthy desires."

This is what happens when we allow envy to invade our hearts. Instead of making decisions out of wisdom, envy causes us to make decisions out of our hurts or out of the desire to prove that we are at or above the same level as others. So, we purchase the car that we know we can't afford to impress others. We take the trip with the money that we should be saving so that we can post the pics on social media. We buy the designer handbag with the money we should be using to pay off our credit card debt. Let me tell ya' that this behavior becomes addictive because you will never feel satisfied. There simply aren't enough shoes, cars, and trips to make you feel as though you are enough.

When we are faced with choices similar to those that Susan made we need to ask ourselves what is driving this decision. "Why is this thing important to me?"

Gratitude has the power to cancel out envy. We must learn to be grateful for the things we do have and what we have accomplished. When we are grateful, it removes our attention from what other people have or don't have to the blessings standing right before us.

The benefits of gratitude are endless; it helps us to foster empathy for others, it builds our self- esteem, and it unleashes our creativity. It also opens the doors to stronger relationships because when we are grateful, we are no longer feeling the need to compete, throw shade, and hate on others, which destroys relationships.

Look around you and take notice of all of the things you have to be grateful for:

- If you have graduated from high school you should be grateful, particularly if your parents did not.
- If you have earned a degree you should be grateful, especially if you have children, because you are teaching them that education is important.
- If you have your own car, you should be grateful.
- If you paid off your car note, you should be grateful.
- If you have a place to live you should be grateful.
- If you are present for your children, you should be grateful.
- If you have traveled outside of your country, you should be grateful.
- If you are healthy, you should be grateful.
- If you have been raped, molested, or assaulted and are now reading this book you should be grateful, because not only are you an overcomer, but you are taking a path to healing and you are still alive and sober in mind to do so. Count your blessings, sis.

Questions to Journal

Have you ever made a purchase or decision to impress others?

_____

_____

_____

_____

_____

_____

_____

Describe any situations where you have felt envious of someone else?

_____

_____

_____

_____

_____

_____

_____

Day 11

Feeling Unloved

Genesis 29:18-30

Now Jacob loved Rachel; so he said, "I will serve you seven years for Rachel, your younger daughter."

And Laban said, "It is better that I give her to you than that I should give her to another man. Stay with me." So Jacob served seven years for Rachel, and they seemed only a few days to him because of the love he had for her.

Then Jacob said to Laban, "Give me my wife, for my days are fulfilled, that I may go in to her." And Laban gathered together all the men of the place and made a feast. Now it came to pass in the evening, that he took Leah his daughter and brought her to Jacob; and he went in to her. And Laban gave his maid Zilpah to his daughter Leah as a maid. So it came to pass in the morning, that behold, it was Leah. And he said to Laban, "What is this you have done to me? Was it not for Rachel that I served you? Why then have you deceived me?"

And Laban said, "It must not be done so in our country, to give the younger before the firstborn. Fulfill her week, and we will give you this one also for the service which you will serve with me still another seven years."

*Then Jacob did so and fulfilled her week. So he gave him his
daughter Rachel as wife also. And Laban gave his
maid Bilhah to his daughter Rachel as a
maid. Then Jacob also went in to Rachel, and he also loved
Rachel more than Leah. And he served with Laban still
another seven years.[1]*

Can you imagine the pain that Leah felt when she discovered
that after she spent the night with Jacob and gave him her
body, he still went to her father asking to marry Rachel? That
had to be devastating! And not only did he still want to marry
Rachel, but he was willing to serve as a slave to Laban for
another seven years! Wow, that's crazy! Rachel must have
been a dime…okurr! In this instance, Leah felt the cold sting
of rejection.

I'm sure this experience made Leah second guess herself, as
rejection often does. I imagine that in Leah's mind she asked
herself, "Was I not good enough for him? Am I not pretty
enough? Was my sex not good enough that he couldn't forget
about her?" This is often how rejection such as this is
internalized.

So, Jacob went on to marry both Rachel and Leah, always
admonishing Rachel as his true love. The Bible says, "Leah
felt unloved." That's the emotion that rejection causes us to
feel - unloved and unlovable.

There are so many things that can occur in our lifetime that
can cause us to take a pause and ask ourselves are we worthy
of love - the mother that compared us to other children, the
husband that has been unfaithful, the father that wasn't
present, the guy that doesn't post any pics of us on his social
media, the adult children that do not visit, the boss that does
not recognize our work, the girlfriend's that do not invite us
to their social events, the guy that treats us as a side piece.
But God does not forget us! Let's look at Genesis 29:

Genesis 29:31-32
When the LORD saw that Leah was unloved, He opened her
womb; but Rachel was barren. So Leah conceived and bore a
son, and she called his name Reuben; for she said,
"The LORD has surely looked on my affliction. Now therefore,
my husband will love me."[1]

We cannot deny that Leah's situation was heartbreaking. She spent most of her life yearning for a man that had very little interest in her. That sucks! But God blessed her to birth many children.

Sis, I firmly believe that there are blessings that have come from rejection. Perhaps you have gained a new perspective, perhaps you have met new friends, perhaps you birthed a child that will bring greatness to the family, perhaps you met the person you were supposed to be with after the lover rejected you, or perhaps you gained new insight and wisdom.

Maybe rejection was God's way of saying He had something better for you. I know that I have looked back at some of my past relationships that went south and thought to myself, "Thank you, Lord for allowing me to dodge that bullet - whew chile!" I've looked back at positions that I had that God moved me from right before the company filed bankruptcy and friendships that were lost that were more harm than good for me. In my mind, I see rejection as God literally pulling us up out of a situation before ish hits the fan and it can truly be a blessing.

We need to begin accepting rejection as it is an inevitable part of life, and look at the benefits that may come with it. Let's not view it as harm, but ask ourselves what are the blessings that are attached to it.

Questions to Journal

Who has rejected you in the past?

_____
_____
_____
_____
_____
_____
_____

How do you feel about the person(s) that you
mentioned above?

_____
_____
_____
_____
_____
_____

How did the rejection make you feel?

_____
_____
_____
_____
_____
_____
_____

Action Item

Have you asked God to help you heal from rejection? If not, write God a letter asking Him to help you release the pain from the rejection.

_____

_____

_____

_____

_____

_____

_____

_____

_____

_____

_____

_____

_____

Vicious Jealousy

James 3:16

For where envy and self-seeking exist, confusion and every evil thing are there.[1]

When we look at the relationship of Leah and Rachel, I'm pretty sure there was jealousy and envy present on both sides. Leah resented Rachel because Jacob really loved her and Rachel resented Leah because she birthed their first child. Both women were looking at the things that the other woman had that they didn't. Jealousy is an interesting emotion because it creeps up on us stealthily. Then, it traps us like an animal in a cage and it won't let us go until it's had its way with us wreaking havoc in our relationships.

Let me explain how this works:

When we meet another sister, or woman, we give her a good ole' once over to see what she has and does not have in comparison to ourselves. We look to see if she is thinner than we are, if she is smarter than we are, if she has a man on her arm, if she is stylish, if she owns a home, if she travels more than we do, and if her home is larger than ours. Then, based on those things, we decide how we are going to treat her. Jealousy is the choice we make when we believe that she is winning in an area that we believe we are lacking. So, we attack her in that area. We begin by making subtle yet shady comments to her such as, "Is that your lil' car?" And we top it off with condescending remarks such as, "I wouldn't want to live in this neighborhood."

We can even become jealous of things unseen that money can't buy such as a person's personality, friendships, power, charisma, and wisdom. It is fine, I suppose, to take notice of these things, but we have entered the realm of jealousy when we allow them to invoke a negative emotion inside of us.

I am involved in many different social groups, community, and faith-based groups. Because of this, I meet lots of women - many that are prettier than I am, more organized than I am, smarter than I am, and that have more stylish tastes than I do. I take notice but I make a choice not to allow jealousy to enter. I love people and making new friends. I don't want to sabotage my relationships by bringing jealousy or envy into it. So, I make it a point to compliment them, praise them for it, and admit that I may lack in that area. I'm very quick to say, "girl, I just loved the way you have decorated your living room. I'm still struggling to decorate mine." Or "sis, your skin is so beautiful. I'm still working on clearing my skin. What products do you use?" This level of vulnerability isn't weakness instead it blocks the jealousy and moves me towards a place of admiration. It also builds a bridge to new relationships because now she knows that I'm not here to compete, but to be a support.

When jealousy sets in, however, we sabotage our relationships by gossiping about them, throwing shade, and desiring the worst for them. Jealousy causes us to secretly want them to fail so that we can win the competition that we have conjured up in our minds.

Many of our disagreements are because jealousy has entered. Many of our relationships fail because we entertain jealousy. Remember, jealousy is a decision. The way we defeat it is by choosing not to be jealous, being content with our own lot in life, and celebrating each other's successes.

Questions to Journal

Do you compare yourself to other women?

_____

_____

_____

_____

_____

_____

_____

What are the things you tend to be the most jealous of?

_____

_____

_____

_____

_____

_____

_____

How do you behave when you are jealous?

_____

_____

_____

_____

_____

_____

_____

Day 13

Taking Things Personally

James 1:19-20
So then, my beloved brethren, let every man be swift to hear, slow to speak, slow to wrath; for the wrath of man does not produce the righteousness of God. [1]

I once had a colleague that I traveled with to California for a week-long training. We had a ball! In the evenings after the training was over, we would hit the town. We visited the Grove and dined at the famous Mr. Chow where we met celebrities. We relaxed on beautiful beaches during lunch while drinking tasty drinks and drove through Malibu looking at all of the gorgeous homes. We had so much fun!

On the last evening, we were driving back to the hotel from dinner. I asked her a question, and she responded in a very curt and snappy manner. My wounded emotions over analyzed it and assumed the worst of her intentions. The following morning, I chose not to meet her for breakfast as I normally did and hopped on my flight leaving Cali without saying goodbye.

After we returned, she tried to reach out to me a few times, but I did not respond. I was done with her. Eventually, she and I both went our separate ways.

My point is that sometimes, we overreact and take things way too personally. I should have given this sister the benefit of the doubt. We had been on the go for an entire week. She was exhausted as was I, so I'm sure that exhaustion was behind her remark. Instead of giving her the benefit of the doubt, I chose to take it personally. I put too much thought into a small matter and made assumptions in my head about her behavior, calling her mean and nasty.

Looking back, there is no one else I would have chosen to go on that trip with other than her. Together, we had so much fun and created many memories together. I can't believe I allowed something so small and harmless to destroy a beautiful friendship. She's human and entitled to make mistakes and as her friend, I needed to extend grace.

Over the years, I have thought about her and tried to find her on social media with no luck. Sis, don't be like me. Please don't take minor things so personally. Always give the benefit of the doubt; always believe the best.

Questions to Journal

Do you take things personally?

_____
_____
_____
_____
_____
_____
_____

What causes you to take things personally?

_____
_____
_____
_____
_____
_____
_____

Describe a situation where you ended a relationship too prematurely?

_____
_____
_____
_____
_____
_____
_____

Those Nasty Grudges

Ephesians 4:32
And be ye kind one to another, tenderhearted, forgiving one
another, even as God for Christ's sake hath forgiven you.[1]

I was once the kind of person that would hold grudges for
years and years. I would retain, in my memory, past events
that have hurt or annoyed me regardless of how minuscule
and when the time was right, I would use it as a weapon. This
was toxic, learned behavior for me.

Many of us create a lifestyle of holding grudges. That's our
way of punishing the people that harm us. Some of us hold
grudges because we do not know other ways to resolve
conflict. We also hold grudges for power and revenge
because we believe we need to hurt the other person, so we
hold on to the hurt and find ways within our means to render
punishment. So, we will ignore the other person, block or
unfriend them on social media, gossip about them, or are
silent when in their presence hoping that this causes them
harm. Our broken heart wants to see them suffer in some
way.

But also, some of us truly believe we have forgiven, yet we
may be still holding on to the emotion attached to the
memory. Although we may say, "I'm over it" yet we truly
haven't let it go. We didn't forgive them; we just hid the pain
for a bit. But, it is in the smallest of misunderstandings that
the hurt will manifest itself. It will cause us to lash out for the
simplest reasons.

We punish ourselves by holding grudges because it makes us bitter. We are also creating a toxic internal environment as holding grudges becomes our tool for fighting battles. In the pit of our hearts rendering poison to our souls, we have grudges piled on top of grudges. Then, once we are triggered, we lash out, releasing all of the rage that we have piled up.

Grudges force us to build walls and those walls choke the life out of our relationships. Because we are still holding on to past hurts, we punish people that enter our lives with the best of intentions for us.

Holding grudges also makes us easily annoyed, easily irritated, and petty. Because we have developed a pattern of holding grudges, our brain cannot discern between the small day to day minor annoyances and the things that need to be added to the pile of grudges we are holding, so it assumes that even the tiniest of annoyances deserves a reaction.

I'm here to tell you that holding grudges harms us and prevents us from having good solid relationships. We have to simply learn to let things go. People are human and will fail us. We have to learn to make peace with this or else we will cause damage to ourselves. There is nothing to gain holding on to hurts but damaged emotions.

Questions to Journal

Do you hold grudges?

_____
_____
_____
_____
_____
_____

If yes, why is it hard to let things go?

_____
_____
_____
_____
_____
_____
_____

Day 15

How Do You Love?

1 Corinthians 13:4-7
Love is patient, love is kind. It does not envy, it does not boast, it is not proud. It does not dishonor others, it is not self-seeking, it is not easily angered, it keeps no record of wrongs. Love does not delight in evil but rejoices with the truth. It always protects, always trusts, always hopes, always perseveres.[1]

Growing up in my family, when one of the children would express that we didn't feel loved the adults would run through a laundry list of all the things they purchased for you. "How dare you say you don't feel loved" they would say. "After all the things we have done for you. You have a house to live in, food, clothing, etc." So, for me, I thought that if someone loves you, they will spend their money on you. Therefore, I began to equate love with money.

We each interpret love differently and many of us love very differently. The way our caregivers loved each other and us, typically impacts how we love. That may not have been a healthy type of love.

The first year or two of my marriage was a struggle. The primary reason was because, often, I tried to force my will on my husband. I wanted him to eat dinner at the time that I wanted him to eat, put the dishes away in the way I wanted him to, and clean the toilets in the way I felt was best. I nagged him constantly. I felt the need to point out his wrong doings, even down to the smallest things, criticizing the way he took out the garbage and how he parked the car in the drive away. As you may have guessed, my behavior caused lots of chaos in our home. But for me, I believed that as long as I was contributing financially to the household that I could behave any way I wanted to. Additionally, I was also acting out on the behavior I saw in my family as I was growing up.

My husband sat me down one day and told me how frustrated he was. I could tell by his tone that he was serious and that this was no ordinary conversation. At that moment, I realized that I don't need to beat him up about everything. No one was getting sick or dying by the way he was taking out the garbage. Truthfully the things that were bothering me were really my own issues not his. I knew I had to learn to be empathetic because I truly loved my husband and didn't want him to resent the decision to marry me or feel as if he was happier when he was single.

I looked at the behavior that my family had embraced and knew it had to change because I wanted something different. Y'all I read 1 Corinthians 13 until I got it in my system! I needed to understand how to love him as well as understand how he wanted to be loved. Not only did I read 1 Corinthians 13, but I studied my husband to understand the things that made him happy and sad. We also had conversations about how we each wanted to be loved.

Now, in our marriage, fourteen years later, I do the things that cause the least amount of chaos in my home. It does not mean I do not speak up, but now I pick my battles and I say things in a way that it doesn't offend. I want peace more than anything in my home, and we are better when we are united.

Questions to Journal

What toxic learned behavior have you embraced that was passed down from your caregivers?

_____

_____

_____

_____

_____

_____

_____

How can you create new positive behaviors to embrace?

_____

_____

_____

_____

_____

_____

_____

_____

Soft Words Win!

Proverbs 15:1
A soft answer turns away wrath, but a harsh word stirs up anger.[1]

"First of all" has become a phrase that I deeply despise. I mean it really grinds my gears. When someone says these words to me with an attitude attached to it, I know that the words following it will be filled with a bunch of drama. Often when someone begins a statement with "first of all" coupled with a defensive tone, my fight or flight response kicks in and I prepare to defend myself. The irony in all of this is that I have used those words myself and it usually does not end well. It is foolish for us to expect to use harsh words or a bad attitude to manage conflict.

When we use harsh words when we are hurt, usually we find ourselves in an argument. What happens when an argument gets intense? We attack and our words become weapons with the intent to hurt and humiliate the person. I used to be queen of this, as it was learned behavior for me. I would hit as far below the belt as I possibly could. Then I would brag about it to my friends, "girl, let me tell you how I checked her." Eventually, I realized that I wasn't winning the argument by doing this. In fact, I was showing how emotionally immature I was and how my wounds were hurting me so bad that I needed to hurt others for a bit of relief.

I read the verse, "a soft answer turns away wrath." It changed my perspective completely. I realized that if I truly wanted to resolve the conflict, instead of "popping off", I need to listen and humble myself. So now when someone does something to hurt me, I take some time to process it, then I come to them with a cool head and a humble tone with the goal of resolution instead of giving them a piece of my mind. This has led to peace for me.

We must decide what we want the outcome to be when we are handling conflict. Giving someone a piece of our mind or telling them off is futile, toxic, and simply a waste of time and energy.

Questions to Journal

Think about the conflicts in your past. How did you handle them?

_____

_____

_____

_____

_____

_____

_____

Have you used your words to hurt someone?

_____

_____

_____

_____

_____

_____

_____

Day 17

Forgiving Me

Micah 7:18-19
"Who is a God like you,
who pardons sin and forgives the transgression
of the remnant of his inheritance?
You do not stay angry forever
but delight to show mercy.
You will again have compassion on us;
you will tread our sins underfoot
and hurl all our iniquities into the depths of the sea."[1]

When I was a young adult, I had an abortion. My immediate
family expressed repeatedly how shameful and embarrassing
it was for me to have sex prior to marriage and, more
importantly, get pregnant. I never truly had a chance to deal
with the actual act of the abortion as my family made sure the
shame was more than enough to punish me.

"You should be ashamed of yourself."

"What a shame!"

"You have brought shame to this family."

This is what I heard consistently. Not once did they ever ask
why I did it or never concerned themselves with what I was
looking for. Instead, they continued to reiterate, how I should
have known better and that they didn't raise me like that.
Then suddenly, the subject was completely dropped.

It didn't really matter how my family felt about the situation. What had the largest impact on my life was how I felt about it. Shame and self-unforgiveness are connected. I realized that I was feeling shame because I had not forgiven myself. The unforgiveness was holding me hostage and wreaking havoc on my life.

Though the abortion was done and over with within a few hours, the shame lasted for years. Let me tell y'all, shame is a robust emotion that gains its strength in our secrecy. We spend our lives holding on to a secret and hoping that no one uncovers it.

Moreover, we may have people in our lives shaming us for all the things we have done wrong, but not one person is showing us how to recover from it. And it's the negative emotions attached to shame, such as fear, embarrassment, humiliation, and guilt that we need freedom from.

Research has proven that shame has the ability to completely change our personality. It causes some to become plagued by feelings of inferiority and inadequacy causing them to become people-pleasers, overly shy, dependent, and many to behave way too submissively. It also forces us to hide and conceal ourselves. Shame prevents us from being who we are supposed to be. [8]

My sis, God forgives us, for everything. Now it's time for you to forgive yourself. If you have shame in your life here are a few keys to healing:

1. **Forgive Yourself -** For some reason, we are able to extend grace and forgiveness to everyone except ourselves. Grieve the experience once more and decide that you will truly let it go. Release it from the very pit of your heart.

2. **Self-Compassion -** We must show ourselves some self-compassion. Understand that you are a human

and flawed, as all of us are, and that your time to heal is now. Understand the circumstances surrounding the choices that you have made. We cannot change the past, but we can change how the past choices impact our future.

3. **Give it Language** - Research has shown that shame causes people to self-conceal and hide.[8] People experiencing shame typically avoid relationships and community because of the fear of being judged. It brings us anxieties because we worry that someone will expose our secrets and if our secret is exposed, we will be judged and no longer be on par with everyone else. You must talk about it and find healthy groups where you can discuss your pain in a safe setting with people that you can trust with your heart. It is in our truth that we are set free.

Please understand that there is no sin, no secret, no choice, and no decision that God is not willing to forgive. There is no decision that we can make that God will not continue his love for us. We must love ourselves though, and extend to ourselves the same grace that God gives.

Questions to Journal

Search you heart and see if you have any areas where forgiveness for yourself is needed. Jot down your thoughts.

_____

_____

_____

_____

_____

_____

_____

Why do you believe you haven't forgiven yourself?

_____

_____

_____

_____

_____

_____

_____

Day 18

You Will Reap What You Sow

Galatians 6:7
Do not be deceived, God is not mocked; for whatever a man
sows, that he will also reap.[1]

There was a guy that I would see often. He was tall,
handsome, with golden brown skin and a huge warm smile.
Charismatic and charming, he often knew the right things to
say at the right time. His stylish clothes always fit his body
perfectly showing off his muscles and swag. He had a great
sense of humor and told the funniest jokes. My close friend
had a crush on him. They would see each other from time to
time, but I wasn't sure if the feelings were mutual between
the two of them. Meanwhile, I was also in a relationship with
someone else.

At a basketball game, he walked behind me and whispered in
my ear, "Girl, you look gorgeous tonight. Let me take you
out for dinner." His words were right on time as they
quenched my thirst for approval and affirmation. I turned
around and smiled back. That was the beginning of our
romantic relationship.

Though I tried to hide it, my friend and boyfriend soon
discovered. Needless to say, it hurt them both. I didn't care. I
had what I wanted. But that relationship proved to me that
what my grandmother always said was true, "you will reap
what you sow."

That relationship was the worst ever - whew chile! In that relationship, he was selfish and a liar. There were always rumors about his infidelities that I had to deal with. Looking back, he was not worth losing a good friendship over and hurting my boyfriend. But at that time, I was selfish as well and had no regard for the feelings of others around me.

One of the things I am pretty sure of is that every single thing we do will return to us, it may not be in the exact same manner, but trust me it will return. If we cause someone hurt or harm, we will face hurt or harm, if we steal something, something will be taken from us. In the same token, if we are kind to others and find opportunities to be a blessing, we will be repaid for that.

Some religions refer to it as karma, others call it "cause and effect", and many others simply chalk it up to "what goes around comes round". Regardless of what it's called reaping and sowing has become the principle that I have built my life around. It works like this: if you plant tomatoes, you can't expect to harvest cucumbers. You must plant or sow what you want to receive or reap.

Trust me when I tell you, if you plant harm or hurt towards others that is what you will get back in life and sometimes it returns to you in double, in ways that you least expect, and often at the worst possible times. Sometimes it can even impact our children. It's so important that we treat everyone with kindness.

As you maneuver through life please make sure you know what you are planting and are prepared to reap it. Ask yourself this simple question: how would I feel if someone treated my child or loved one the same way I acted?

Questions to Journal

List five things that are important to you.

_____
_____
_____
_____
_____
_____
_____
_____

What type of seeds do you need to plant or sow to receive those things?

_____
_____
_____
_____
_____
_____
_____
_____

The God that Loves Black Girls

John 3:16
For God so loved the world that He gave His only
begotten Son, that whoever believes in Him should not perish
but have everlasting life.[1]

It is sometimes difficult for Black Girls to believe in Jesus or
the Bible and I completely understand the reasons why.
Taken out of context, the Bible was used to enslave us – the
"us" being Black people. Our beloved ancestors were raped,
beaten, tortured, and disenfranchised by people that believed
that this was the will of God.

In school, we learned of Europeans that imperialized the
world using a version of Christianity that would keep many
people in bondage and removed from their native land. The
Bible has been used to justify a system in which many people
were deemed inferior based on race.

Many of our places of worship were decorated with pictures
of a Jesus that looked just like those persons that enslaved us.
This left us searching for a higher power that we could
identify with.

Moreover, many of us grew up under the hand of a Big
Momma that used the Bible to keep us in line. She would tell
us all the things we were doing wrong and how our actions
would send us to hell. She introduced us to a God that would
give and take away his salvation from us like a parent would
take away something from a child that misbehaved for not
getting their way.

And if I can be honest, going to church was an all-day production that was boring, whew chile!! Each Sunday sitting on hard pews watching on as the congregation sang what felt like sixty hymns, then the secretary making hundreds of random announcements, and finally the pastor spouting a long-winded sermon that you really didn't understand, and the regulars took their turns vying for attention, shouting, hooping, and hollering.

On top of that, we soon began to discover that many of the beloved leaders in our churches held secrets and lived different lives outside of church. We discovered them doing all of the things that they told us not to do, Sunday after Sunday.

Many churches had stiff rules particularly for women - no jewelry, no skirts above the knee, and no make-up. They were tough on women, beating modesty and submission into our heads and some even told us we couldn't be leaders. All of these things tainted our views.

I remember being in my early twenties and thinking I don't want this salvation because it is too hard. I felt I would always make mistakes and never be perfect. It also seemed like it would require me to live a dull life constantly worrying about all the things I should not be doing. This was also around the time that I began to meet people that were practicing other religions, so I became curious about their faiths. By the time I was 24 and a working professional, I made a promise to myself that I would never spend another Sunday in a two to three hour church service.

The irony in all of this was that during this time, everywhere I seemed to go, I felt Jesus beckoning me. I would be waiting for the bus at the bus stop when suddenly several girls would walk up to me and ask me to visit their church. At work, there would be a co-worker that could sense when I was having a bad day and they'd share a scripture with me. I would have dreams of Jesus talking to me. This thing just would not leave me alone!

It was also during this time that life happened. I lost my job and had no money because I did not save well. I was miles away from family and honestly I did not want to tell them my problems for fear of being judged. My closest friends helped as much as they could, but we were all just starting out in our careers. I had no one to depend on but Jesus. I had attended church all of my life and a private Christian school, but I did not know how to pray. So I simply said, "Jesus if you are real, I need help." Let me tell you that this season became one of the best seasons of my life. I became so close to God and literally watched Jesus answer prayer after prayer.

At that time, I decided I wanted to understand Christianity for myself. I began reading and studying the Bible, attending church (one that only lasted for an hour and fifteen minutes). I grew so interested, that I started taking Biblical courses and became involved in serving in the church. Many blessings came from this, such as making life-long friends and meeting my husband of now fourteen years.

Three things I want you to understand from all of this:

*Understand who Jesus is for yourself. Study and read for yourself and ask Him to reveal Himself to you.

*What Jesus wants more than anything is for you to have a personal relationship with Him. It's not about what we wear, what we eat, or what we listen to. It's about accepting Him and giving our hearts to Him.

*People are flawed individuals, including Christian leaders. Many are irrational and make mistakes that go against the values that they teach. Their actions should never take away from our relationship with Christ.

Questions to Journal

What is your view of God?

_____
_____
_____
_____
_____
_____
_____
_____

What is your view of Jesus?

_____
_____
_____
_____
_____
_____
_____

What has shaped your view of God and Jesus?

_____
_____
_____
_____
_____
_____
_____
_____

Who is Jesus to You?

Matthew 16-13-18
When Jesus came into the region of Caesarea Philippi, He
asked His disciples, saying, "Who do men say that I, the Son
of Man, am?"

So they said, "Some say John the Baptist, some Elijah, and
others Jeremiah or one of the prophets."

He said to them, "But who do you say that I am?"

Simon Peter answered and said, "You are the Christ, the Son
of the living God."

Jesus answered and said to him, "Blessed are you, Simon
Bar-Jonah, for flesh and blood has not revealed this to you,
but My Father who is in heaven. And I also say to you
that you are Peter, and on this rock I will build My church,
and the gates of Hades shall not prevail against it.[1]

Picture it: A King that sits on a throne in a beautiful space
filled with joy and happiness. He is worshiped day and night.
He leaves the comforts of His space to visit earth to help and
save humankind.

He wasn't born in the comforts of anything similar to a
modern hospital, but yet he was born in a stable of sorts
surrounded by hay, loud animal noises and the smell of
animal feces. Earth, mud, and hay was used for cushion and
to cover Him.

This King walked the earth and experienced all forms of grief and sorrow as He saw mankind strive for riches and significance while He, who came to love and receive them, was rejected and ridiculed. The final blow—being beaten to the point of death in front of His dear mother. This King was none other than the one we call Jesus.

It strikes me that Jesus would ask His followers, "who do men say I am? Who do you say I am?" I'm sure Jesus was not suffering from some strange form of identity crisis or amnesia. He was certainly too young for dementia. But I've come to believe that He was asking, "Who am I to you?"

Let me give you an example to illustrate my thoughts: my husband and I both have a relationship with our daughter. To me, I see her as a feisty, inquisitive, know-it-all-ish eight-year-old. For my husband, he sees her as a sweet, sensitive, humble, sharp, and observant child. Our relationship with her determines our perception of her and our perception of her determines how we receive and respond to her. I often find myself trying to redirect her while feeding her curiosity. My husband, on the other hand, is much more gentle and patient with her than I am.

So, it is with Jesus, as we begin developing a relationship with Him, He will begin to reveal himself to us. How do we develop a relationship with Him, you ask? Just as we develop a relationship with anyone else—by talking to Him (prayer) and spending time with Him and learning more about Him (reading the Bible). You should never let anyone define your relationship with Jesus. You have the ability to develop a relationship with Him for yourself that is distinct and different from others.

Questions to Journal

Describe your relationship with Jesus?

_____

_____

_____

_____

_____

_____

_____

_____

_____

_____

_____

_____

_____

Action Item

In your prayer time, ask Jesus to reveal Himself to you.

WCAP

Song of Songs 7:1-3

How beautiful are your feet in sandals,
O prince's daughter!
The curves of your thighs are like jewels,
The work of the hands of a skillful workman.
Your navel is a rounded goblet;
It lacks no blended beverage.
Your waist is a heap of wheat
Set about with lilies.
Your two breasts are like two fawns,
Twins of a gazelle.[1]

My eight-year-old asked me one day out of the blue, "What is sex?" As you can imagine, I almost fell out of my chair onto the floor. However, I promised myself that whenever my children had questions about sex or anything for that matter, I would give them the age-appropriate truth.

For me growing up, my family overreacted when I asked questions about sex and the only answers I could get were, "Don't do it and certainly don't get pregnant. It will be embarrassing if you get pregnant." So there was always a shame attached to sex for me because of their reaction.

As I grew older, I began to do my own research and form my own opinions. I realized that God created sex. And he created it to be enjoyable, not some bore fest. Hence the reason why our body secretes dopamine, the pleasure chemical, when we have sex. I began to seek to understand sex from God, our creator's perspective, so I read the entire book of the Bible referred to as the Song of Solomon and studied each line. In these passages, King Solomon loved his bride, and they had a night of sensual sex. I mean they really got it in!!

Issues arise when we have sex irresponsibly. Ladies, we must be honest with ourselves; there have been times when we have used sex to gain love. We have used sex to feel valued and loved. We have used sex to gain money or status. We have also used sex to hide from the pain of love lost. And most of us could have prevented some of our hurts by not engaging in sex.

For women, sex is mostly emotional. There must be some form of attraction present, whether physical, emotional, or superficial, in order to engage in sex. We often view sex as connection and during those sensual moments, in our minds, we believe he is ours, regardless of what is going on in his world.

More importantly, for women, a hormone called oxytocin is released in the body when we have physical sex. This hormone is associated with bonding, trust, and loyalty. This is often why we become emotionally attached after engaging in sex.

For men, on the other hand, as we all know, many do not need to have any type of emotional connection to engage in sex. I can recall as a kid overhearing a conversation between my older cousins, "She has a big booty, I'm gonna smash that." "She's fine! I can't wait to tap that." For some men, it's not always about the emotional connection rather, they are chasing the feeling they get from sex as well as the ego boost they gain from conquering their conquest. This is one of the reasons we are ghosted after we have sex because for them it was just sex.

Today, women are feeling much more empowered to engage in casual sex. Female Hip Hop Artists such as Cardi B and Megan Thee Stallion are removing the stigma and shame from the word "hoe". Television shows such as *Insecure* show us that casual sex provides us with no backlash. My concern is that this causes people to view sex as trivial; it's just a means to get a good feeling, to bust a nut. But, my sisters, please understand that sex is so much more than that.

Let's understand what happens when we engage in sex.

Our totality consists of three layers:

Body - Our physical self. The layer that can be experienced through all the senses

Soul - Our mind, will, and emotions

Spirit - Our true selves and the part of us that survives after death. Our connection to God and the spirit realm. The part of us that communicates with God.[10]

Because sex is one of the highest levels of connection one can engage in, through our genitals, our entire beings intertwine-- body, soul, and spirit. For this reason, we may notice significant changes after having sex because not only are we exchanging bodily fluids, but we are also exchanging emotions, emotional reactions, positive and negative energy, and spiritual wounds.[10] For example, I recall after having sex with a guy I was dating in my twenties. He was the type of guy that was desperate for material possessions and would do almost anything to gain lots of money. After our relationship ended, I noticed that I began to have similar desires. I lusted for things and the more things I had the more they never seemed to be enough. Not only that, but I began to attract both intimately and platonically people that were consumed with similar traits--various versions of lust. I can recall meeting a new friend that wanted to have sex with anyone and anything walking at any time because lust has no limits and can never wait. I began attracting people that were outside of my norm because, just as magnets, spirits attract like spirits.

"...with every stroke I am receiving in a spirit of an unlikely stranger." Whit D. posted in her blog on celibacy in 2016. She is highlighting the transferring of energy, which many sexologists agree occurs during sexual intimacy.[10] Author and teacher, Netisha Alie explains it as, "With the high level of connection that can be felt in the body based on how much it changes and releases, it is obvious that each person is 'depositing' their energies into the other through the connection of the genitals. This is where the two really become one..." Sickness and diseases are just the visible transfers that everyone accepts. However, attitudes (i.e., spirits; emotions, etc.) as previously mentioned, are all vibrational energies that are being transferred into the other person." [11]

These are soul ties and it's a very real thing. As painful as it is to believe it, after sexual intercourse, you are not completely free of that person. Through sex, they have left a mark on you that can impact you in a very negative manner.

Here's how you know you may have a soul tie with a previous lover:

*You had sex with him years ago, but he's still on your mind.

*You have dreams about him.

*You compare your present lovers to him.

*You see a stranger and you are instantly reminded of him.

*You see a couple in a movie or on a TV show, and they remind you of your relationship with him.

*You get the butterfly feeling in your stomach when someone mentions his name.

*You keep up with them via social media and friends

If you answered yes to any of the above statements, it means that person has invaded your soul, and they are firmly implanted in your mind and emotions. The night you spent with them has come and gone, but they are in your heart and mind for years to come.

For this reason, God encourages us to wait until marriage before we have sex. Now listen, before you toss this book out of the window, I know I sound like a prude. I mean, who doesn't want to have lots of good sex, married or not. And I'm certainly not here to tell you that abstinence is a piece of cake. Trust me, I've been there. But I do want you to understand that there is a cost that we must pay. I think about the heartache I could have spared myself at the expense of dumb dudes if sex had not skewed my view. And honestly, soul ties do have an impact on our marriage. I find it interesting that we choose not to obey God in this manner but yet we want Him to bless our marriages.

God does not want us to engage in sex before marriage because He does not want us to have fun, it's because He wants to protect our hearts and our future. He also wants sex to be enjoyable and amazing just as it was for Solomon and his new wife. King Solomon not only had sex with his wife, but he was intimate with her, carefully enjoying every part of her body, and never once asking her to do anything that would make her feel less than a queen.

Pray and ask God to help you get rid of those soul ties and do all you can to prevent future ones from occurring.

Questions to Journal

Have you had sex with someone that you really liked but the feeling was unrequited?

_____
_____
_____
_____
_____
_____
_____

If you are unmarried, how can you assure God blesses your future marriage? If you are currently married how can you make your sex life is even better?

_____
_____
_____
_____
_____
_____
_____

Do you believe you have any soul ties?

_____
_____
_____
_____
_____

Action Item

If you said yes to having a soul tie, let's take steps to break the soul tie.

1. Acknowledge the soul ties that you have

2. Get rid of anything that you have that belongs to or is from that person (i.e., t-shirts, pictures, text messages, social media, DMs, etc.)

3. Renounce any commitments or vows made that played a part in forming the soul tie. Even things like "I will never a find another like you", "You are the best", "I will love you forever", or "I could never love another man!" need to be renounced. They are spoken commitments that need to be undone verbally.

4. Forgive that person if you have anything against them.

5. Pray and ask God to help you release the soul tie

Day 22

Setting the Captives Free!

Ephesians 4:7-10

But to each one of us grace was given according to the measure of Christ's gift. Therefore, He says:

"When He ascended on high,
He led captivity captive,
And gave gifts to men."

(Now this, "He ascended"—what does it mean but that He also first descended into the lower parts of the earth? He who descended is also the One who ascended far above all the heavens, that He might fill all things.)[1]

This is a powerful passage. It's so profound that I want to spend two days delving into it. This passage explains Jesus' ascension to heaven from the pits of hell. After His death, He descended into hell and "held captivity captive". Captivity is defined as the condition of being confined or imprisoned. So, this passage tells us that Jesus went to hell to take captive all the things on this earth that have the ability to hold us captive; sickness, disease, emotional trauma, depression, anxiety, etc.

We have the power through Christ to have dominion over those things instead of them having dominion over us. Having dominion may come in various forms - it may be changing your lifestyle, changing your diet, medication, seeing a therapist, prayer, etc. But pray and allow God to lead you to what is right for you. And remember that God is in everything including therapy and medication.

My grandmother was diagnosed with colon cancer in 1994. The doctor told her that she would only have 6 months to a year left to live and encouraged her to be put on a treatment of chemotherapy. As a family, we began to prepare for her death. After carefully praying about it, she decided to refuse the chemo and to try a more holistic approach. She changed her diet completely and began to add herbs, organic fruits and veggies to her diet (this was before this type of lifestyle was a thing). She eliminated red meat and sugar from her diet. Because of these changes, my grandmother surpassed the doctor's expectations and lived for 12 more years passing away in 2006, the same year that I got married. In addition, because she refused the chemo, she did not spend her final days filled with lots of pain that is often a side effect of chemo. My point is, pray to God and seek His direction for all the things that are holding you captive.

Questions to Journal

What are things that may be holding you captive?

_____

_____

_____

_____

_____

_____

_____

_____

We Move Differently

Ephesians 4:7-10

But to each one of us grace was given according to the measure of Christ's gift. Therefore, He says:

"When He ascended on high,
He led captivity captive,
And gave gifts to men."

(Now this, "He ascended"—what does it mean but that He also first descended into the lower parts of the earth? He who descended is also the One who ascended far above all the heavens, that He might fill all things.)[1]

Grace is defined as *"simple elegance or refinement of movement."*[13]

As you are healing your wounds, learning to control your emotions instead of allowing them to control you, and allowing God's grace to reign in your life, you will begin to see things in a very different light; your world view will change. Some of the things that used to upset you, you will be able to shrug off. The behaviors that you used to embrace you will now release. Rage developed from your wounds will no longer have their way with you. You may no longer desire to argue, fuss, fight, self-sabotage and curse people out anymore. Peace and grace will become your umpires.

Additionally, the things that used to scare you, you will now be prepared and able to face head on. Fear will no longer hold you back. You will begin to draw a completely different tribe towards you because your energy will be different. People will look at you and say, "that sis moves differently!"

Having said that, be aware that some people will dislike you, hate you, dismiss you, and even leave your side. Please understand that it's not you they are disapproving of, it's the light inside of you and the emotional healthy life that you now lead that they resent. You see, misery loves company, but resents healing. There are some people that have been exposed to darkness and toxic behavior for so long that an emotionally healthy person is foreign to them. They do not want to experience the light that is inside of you because it requires change and change is frightening to them. Toxicity, however, is comfortable for them.

In the book of Genesis, one of the first things that God did when He created all that we know as our universe, was to separate light from darkness. They are very distinct and have completely different purposes; daylight is used to help things grow, to help us see, and to give life to all living things through the nutrients transmitted from the sun. Darkness, on the other hand, is used for sleep, and many have used it to hide, conceal, and to experience sadness. It is for your good to be separated from people that are not willing to heal. Everyone can't go where you are going and travel where you will.

I was deeply hurt when I saw that some people whom I deeply loved completely wrote me off. Some even hated me for no real reason. They berated me when I walked away from fights and toxic behavior and for standing up for peace in my home. They didn't understand how I loved and submitted to my husband and encouraged me to do the opposite. I was crushed but I learned to accept it. I want to encourage you, my dear sis, to learn early on to accept this and, more importantly, embrace the people that love and support your journey to healing. There you will find your tribe.

Questions to Journal

Think of someone that you know or may have met that moves in an emotionally healthy manner?

_____

_____

_____

_____

_____

_____

_____

What, specifically, is it about them that you admire?

_____

_____

_____

_____

_____

_____

_____

There is Purpose in our Pain

Romans 8:28
And we know that all things work together for good to those
who love God, to those who are the called according
to His purpose.[1]

It was a warm early fall evening. I had recently moved to the Washington, DC area and was living with my aunt in Silver Spring, MD. A friend had invited me to attend a Bible study at one of the largest churches in Prince George's County Maryland. Now to be honest with you, my first thought was, "can't we meet at happy hour instead? It's Two Dollar Tuesdays at Club Dream!" But my friend insisted and I had no other plans for that evening, so I agreed and met her there.

When I arrived, I noticed there was a different vibe as I was entering this church. There was a feeling of excitement in the air, which is rare for a Tuesday night Bible study, in my experience. Additionally, the church was packed just as if it was a Sunday morning service. We could barely find a seat.

As the service began, everyone pulled out their Bibles, notebooks, pens and highlighters, and were ready to learn. This Bible study proved to be unlike any Bible study I had ever attended. The ones I previously attended in my hometown were attended only by a few much older people and seemed to be an utter bore.

At this Bible study, the pastor's message was delightful as it was a combination of real life anecdotes, comedy, and Biblical wisdom like I've never heard before. Each illustration gave a full well-rounded understanding of the message that I found relatable in so many ways.

Particularly, there was one thing that I heard on that night that stood out to me like a fat sore thumb. It would be the key point that I learned from that night that my soul would carry with me for the remainder of my life. It would also be the words that I clung to during the darkest of times: *"And we know that all things work together for good to them that love God, to them who are the called according to his purpose."* At that moment, these words changed my entire life. I guess this is what auntie Oprah would refer to as an aha moment.

I have experienced a lot of emotional trauma. From toxic relationships and rejection, to dysfunctional family, to poor friendships that hurt me, to battling anxiety as well as my own insecurities. Those hurts still dwelt inside of me and had jaded my perception. But when I heard those words it was as if I was struck by lightning. At that moment, I realized that ALL of my experiences were for a purpose. There was a bigger reason for the pain.

Today, my husband and I counsel married couples that are in crisis, I counsel women that are hurting, and I have written books about my journey toward emotional healing. In each of those areas, I have had to use my painful past to relate and empathize with the people that I am helping. That is the beauty of God. He makes sense of our pain!

Sis, I am here to tell you that it does not matter what you have been through in life, God can use it for a greater purpose. Ask Him to reveal that to you. Understand that everyone has a purpose but it will not reveal itself to you until you are ready for it to prevent you from abusing it or mishandling it. It takes wisdom and self-control to carry out purpose. There is no need to run from your pain, run to it. Understand it, resolve it, and use it to help others.

Questions to Journal

What are the two most painful incidents that have
occurred in your life?

_____

_____

_____

_____

_____

_____

_____

How can you use those painful incidents to help
others?

_____

_____

_____

_____

_____

_____

_____

Day 25

We are Put Here to do More Than Get Fly

John 18:6-10
When Jesus had spoken these words, He went out with His
disciples over the Brook Kidron, where there was a garden,
which He and His disciples entered. And Judas, who betrayed
Him, also knew the place; for Jesus often met there with His
disciples. Then Judas, having received a detachment of
troops, and officers from the chief priests and Pharisees, came
there with lanterns, torches, and weapons. Jesus
therefore, knowing all things that would come upon Him,
went forward and said to them, "Whom are you seeking?"
They answered Him, "Jesus of Nazareth." Jesus said to
them, "I am He." And Judas, who betrayed Him, also stood
with them. Now when He said to them, "I am He," they drew
back and fell to the ground.

Imagine, Jesus being face to face with soldiers who are about
to brutally murder Him. In this moment, He is also standing
face to face with the man that was His friend, and was
amongst His very trusted circle. This same friend betrayed
Jesus for money—that friend's name was Judas.

When the soldiers asked for Him, Jesus responds with three small words, "I am He." But He says it in such a way that they literally fell to the ground. Those words obviously packed some power! This demonstrates the power of knowing and being confident in who we are. Jesus knew who His father was, He knew what His purpose was, and He knew that His purpose would have a greater impact than the moment He was faced with.

One of the keys to being confident is connecting with a purpose far bigger than ourselves. Purpose consists of having an impact on others and thinking of and considering things outside of ourselves for something bigger than ourselves. For example, in just thirty short years, Jesus healed the sick, raised people from the dead, fed the hungry, taught, recruited and trained staff, turned water into bomb wine, died, went to hell, and was resurrected. Over 2000 years later, Jesus is still widely discussed around the world by both believers and non-believers. Now that is a purpose filled life! So, when He stood face to face with his enemies, Jesus knew who He was and what He brought to the table and that's where He derived His power, not in empty possessions or accolades. Purpose has power!

But here is the key—everything He did on earth made an impact on other people

At the intersection of our hurts, skills, and talents, we find our purpose. And often it may include sharing our story or using our past hurts to help others. That's why sharing our story is so powerful—there is purpose in our story! We gain confidence every time we use our story to help others.

Continue to ask God to reveal your purpose to you. You can also look for purpose in the everyday things you enjoy doing such as sharing wisdom with your children, hosting events in your home that make people feel comfortable, and cheering up those that are down. Pay attention to the things that you enjoy doing as they may be pointing you to something bigger.

Questions to Journal

What are your skills and talents?

_____

_____

_____

_____

_____

_____

_____

_____

What are some things that deeply interest you?

_____

_____

_____

_____

_____

_____

_____

If you could do any job in the world (money is not an option) and you knew you would be successful at it, what would it be?

_____

_____

_____

_____

_____

_____

_____

*Action Items

Ask five (5) of your closest friends and family members what they believe you are good at.

Find two (2) people that you trust to share your personal story with. Document how you feel afterwards over the next few days.

Day 26

She Can't Keep A Man

Jeremiah 29:11
"For I know the thoughts that I think toward you, says
the LORD, thoughts of peace and not of evil, to give you a
future and a hope."[1]

"She can't keep a man," "She can't get a man," "He doesn't want her." These are words that I have heard black girls say about each other. And, to be honest, I have said these words myself or agreed with them. These words send a message that we are not valuable if we are not on a man's arm. Because of that, when we are not in a relationship, we wonder, "why hasn't a man chosen me?" "What's wrong with me?" "Am I too thick?" "Am I too successful?" "Am I too cautious?" "Am I pretty enough?" It tears apart our self-esteem. What's worse is that it can force us to settle to prevent the unspoken judgement, to please everyone else, and to prove our worth.

Growing up, I witnessed women surrendering to lots of torment from men. Some men held secrets, some lived double lives, some gambled away the family finances, others did hard drugs while many just would not come home at night. But in each scenario, the women either ignored the red flags and married them anyway or stayed far longer than expected. That's often what happens when the apex of our lives is being in a relationship.

I can remember the first time I read the words in Jeremiah 29:11, *"For I know the thoughts that I think toward you, says the LORD, thoughts of peace and not of evil, to give you a future and a hope."[1]* I knew then that some of the men that I had been dating represented evil for me and were not a reflection of the peace and hope God wanted for me. The things that I had tolerated from men – the ego, the selfishness, the cheating, the lies, the disrespect were a mirror of my own fears and concerns about being single. Sis, having a man on your arm does NOT equate to happily ever after. If you select the wrong partner, it can make your life a living nightmare.

We must defeat loneliness and that includes becoming comfortable being alone with ourselves before we can expect anyone else to want to be with us. You are your best friend! Additionally, we need to be emotionally mature and value ourselves before we are ready to receive a long-term partner. Valuing ourselves begins with understanding who we are, what we stand for, and developing healthy boundaries and criteria based on that.

Single ladies, please hear me when I say this, if your list of attributes that you are looking for in a mate includes any of the following: height requirements, swag, the way he dresses, what he does for a living, the fraternity he is in, or the type of car he drives please do yourself a favor and remain single. This is a true indicator that you are not emotionally or mentally ready to tackle marriage. Those things are superficial and have absolutely nothing to do with the way he treats you, the way he loves you, the way he respects you, his ability to make decisions, and his ability to be faithful to you. If you focus on superficial things you will find yourself disappointed and frustrated because you neglected to focus on things that matter. And as you evolve and grow, your desires will change and you will soon realize that you are in a relationship with someone for all the wrong reasons and you are with someone that is perfectly mismatched for you.

We can also get so used to dating a certain type of guy that we truly believe those toxic and superficial things are important. We date the street guy, the thug, the irresponsible guy, the emotionally unavailable guy because he is cute and that's what we are accustomed to dating. And often, that is the only type we believe we have the ability to attract. Yet we call the guy that is emotionally healthy and self-controlled "corny" simply because his behavior is foreign to us. Therefore, to us, it makes him appear less desirable.

An emotionally mature woman looks at how a man spends his money, his relationship with God BEFORE he met you, how he treats other people (even his baby momma), who his friends are, how he takes care of his kids, how much self-control he has, how hard he works, what drives him, and how he handles being offended. Those are the things that are found in the heart of a person, and more importantly, those are the things that will have the greatest impact on your life.

Questions to Journal

In looking at Jeremiah 29:11, "*For I know the thoughts that I think toward you, says the* LORD, *thoughts of peace and not of evil, to give you a future and a hope,*"[1] what are some things in your life that are evil and not peaceful?

_____

_____

_____

_____

_____

_____

_____

_____

Day 27

Guard your Heart, Sis

Proverbs 4:23
Keep your heart with all diligence,
For out of it spring the issues of life.[1]

I can recall in my early twenties when I first moved to DC that I began dating a guy. He was active-duty military and stationed in the area. At the beginning, I believe it was our 2nd or 3rd date, and we were driving in traffic. The I-495 beltway is known for heavy traffic particularly at certain times of the day. At any rate, we were headed to the movie theater when we got stuck in traffic. While sitting, a car cut us off. He grew angry and yelled some harsh words at the driver. The driver yelled back with obscenities. My boyfriend's anger intensified and before I knew it, he was waving for the driver of the other car to pull over, so they could battle it out. That was my first red flag and revelation of what was to come. But because he was handsome, available, had a good job, and without a lot of baggage, I remained in that relationship.

As things progressed, I realized he was emotionally scarred and angry. He was rude, at times, and even rude to my friends that truly loved me. He was quick to overreact and to fly off the handle. He would be ready to end the relationship at the slightest annoyances. And his spending habits, whew! He would easily spend sixty dollars on drinks alone at dinner, yet complain when he was broke the following week. He always wanted to have his way and didn't have much regard for my boundaries, but was adamant about me respecting his.

I should have ran at the first red flag. But I didn't. I stayed. I assumed he would be better because I was lonely. I assumed this was okay because I liked the idea of being in a relationship. I also believed it proved I had value - because someone valued me. When the relationship ended, I was hurt and all the toxic things that I experienced with him made me toxic.

My point is, ladies, as cliché as it sounds, we need to guard our hearts. And guarding our hearts means we need to be emotionally whole enough to leave at the first sight of toxic behavior —before we become too emotionally invested. Let me tell you that you demonstrate your power when you walk away! Like cancer, some relationships can poison our souls making us emotionally sick. We need to realize we have total control over our hearts and what and who we allow into it. Keep your eyes wide open and ask yourself, "If this person does not change, can I live with the worst of their behavior for the rest of my life?" "Am I my best self when I'm in a relationship with this person?"

Now sis, if you do choose to stay, that's your right and your decision. You still need to guard your heart by selecting boundaries that will protect you from being hurt. After you select boundaries have a discussion with your partner about them letting him firmly know what you will and will not accept. Stick to them and maintain them. Anyone that does not value you for having boundaries and does not honor your boundaries, doesn't truly value all of you.

Questions to Journal

Describe a relationship, romantic partner, or friendship that was toxic for you?

_____
_____
_____
_____
_____
_____
_____

Why did you remain in that relationship?

_____
_____
_____
_____
_____
_____

List the boundaries that you have that help to guard your heart?

_____
_____
_____
_____
_____
_____
_____

Good Friends

---

1 Corinthians 15:33
Do not be misled: "Bad company corrupts good character."[1]

I am a very open and genuine person. I love hard and go hard for my friends. Because of my openness, I have allowed many people to enter my sacred space and some of those people have not been for me. This is, quite frankly, my weakness. I have suffered lots of heartache because of this. I have learned, the very hard way, that everyone is not meant to wear the title of friend. Just as God will send people into our life to love us and help us grow, the devil, our adversary, will send people in our lives to trick us, deceive us, distract us, and hurt us.

We have to learn the intricacies of people, just as we would when dating, before we allow them to enter our sacred spaces. We need to understand who they are, what motivates them, what angers them, how they behave when they are angry, how rational their thinking is, what their belief system is, and more importantly, what their unhealed wounds are and assure that all of those things align with our world view and the direction we are headed. There are some people that are put in our lives to hold us back and prevent us from fulfilling our purpose.

We need to understand how they define friendship because we are not all on the same page when it comes to friendship. It takes time to cultivate true friendships. It also takes surviving the tests. Our friendships must experience and survive conflict and tough moments. Those are the moments that define and deepen our friendships.

In the Bible, Jesus had numerous associates but John, however, is referenced no fewer than five times as the one that Jesus loved. John was tortured and boiled alive and still never denied Jesus. The mark of a true friend is if they defend your name behind your back. Pay attention to see if the people that you refer to as friends have the courage to defend you or if they become weak and engage in the gossip about you.

Before his death, John was exiled to the island of Patmos. It was there that Jesus visited him, comforted him, and revealed to him the book of Revelation. I love their relationship because it is very reciprocal, with both men giving and receiving. They are both equally invested in the friendship.

Their friendship also shows us that true friends provide us comfort when we need it and bring us a source of peace. Friends that are too preoccupied with themselves and their own world to comfort us or friends that bring us a bunch of drama have no place in our hearts.

Finally, it takes vulnerability to deepen our relationships. It is the mutual sharing of our hearts, pains, and fears that develops true friendship. Someone that genuinely wants to be in friendship with you will remove the guards to let you in to get to know their "real". This means that trust is present. Please understand that once we lose the trust of a friend, the relationship becomes superficial and may eventually die. When someone trusts us with their heart it is our responsibility to do all we can to protect and preserve that trust.

Questions to Journal

List the close friends that you have where you mutually defend and show up for each other and are both vulnerable within the relationship?

_____

_____

_____

_____

_____

_____

_____

Is there anyone in your life that you believe may serve as a distraction for you?

_____

_____

_____

_____

_____

_____

_____

Day 29

Can You Handle The Real?

Proverbs 1:7
The fear of the LORD is the beginning of knowledge; But fools despise wisdom and instruction.[1]

My husband's profession typically calls for him to work in various locations. From day to day, he can be found walking through highly secured locations across the US. Often, he bumps into a few of the older gentlemen from our previous church that mentored him earlier in our marriage. Not only will they inquire as to how he is doing, but they will do somewhat of an ad hoc check up to gauge the health of our marriage. "Are you still being the leader of your home?", they ask. This is the essence of accountability.

Accountability is difficult for many of us to accept. We shy away from it because we do not want people "in our business" and I get that. Additionally, our insecurities fear that someone will tell us we are wrong. But we need to have some accountability in our lives. Someone should be able to tell you when you are wrong and assure that you are still on the right path. Without accountability, there is no growth or wisdom, and we will likely make decisions that cause us harm.

How many times have you asked someone for advice, but you really did not want their wisdom, you wanted someone to confirm what you already felt or believed? Should I marry him? Should I buy this home? Should I take this job? You ask the question, but do you get frustrated if someone tells you something different from what you expected to hear? This typically means you are emotionally invested in one particular course of action. We have to learn to take our emotions out of situations and brace ourselves for the truth. If you have gone to them for advice or they are in close enough proximity to you to extend advice, it means you must have some level of trust for them.

The beginning of wisdom is understanding that we may be wrong. This is hard to embrace sometimes because we often want to be right. We want things to go our own way. We want what we want when we want it. But please believe me when I tell you that "No" may be the best thing for you. It may be preventing you from a world of chaos and trouble. Keep people with wisdom and a love for God in your life and always remove your emotions until you hear God give you a clear "Yes". When God gives us a "Yes", He does so without repentance and He confirms it over and over again.

How do we hear God, you ask? Here are some ways:

*He speaks to us through family, friends, and other loved ones.

*He speaks to us through a sermon or preached word.

*He speaks to us through circumstances such as closed doors.

*He speaks to us through a dream or vision.

*He speaks to us through the Bible and Christian literature.

*He speaks to us through the still small uncontrollable voice in our hearts during our silence.

Questions to Journal

List three people in your life that provide wisdom and advice to you.

_____

_____

_____

_____

_____

_____

_____

Have you heard God speak to you?

_____

_____

_____

_____

_____

_____

If yes, how has God spoken to you?

_____

_____

_____

_____

_____

_____

The Day I Learned to Love My Father

Psalm 68:5-6
A father of the fatherless, a defender of widows,
Is God in His holy habitation.
God sets the solitary in families;
He brings out those who are bound into prosperity;
But the rebellious dwell in a dry land.[1]

My father was not in my life. Although I had a wonderful step-father, grandfather, and uncles, my biological father's absence was felt. By his lack of presence, he established the template for relationships for me. Therefore, during my early dating experiences, I managed to attract emotionally unavailable men.

I also had a front row seat as I watched some of the other men in my family behave unfaithfully to their wives and girlfriends. Therefore, that is what I expected of men when I began dating. I attracted what I knew.

But at some point, I grew tired, y'all. Sick and tired. I decided I needed a change. I refused to bring children into this world by a man that resembled my father, I didn't want that for them. But I really did not know what a good husband and father truly looked like.

I had to understand that God was my father. And His grace and mercy towards me was better than anything on earth. I learned to love God just as I would my earthly father. When I embraced God's love and goodness, I began to see the standard He set in terms of men. I began to desire love that resembled God's love. Therefore, subconsciously, I went from attracting men like my absent father to men that are more like my heavenly father - kind, gentle, faithful, responsible, present, available, forgiving, wise, and warm. You see, I firmly believe that men can tell when a woman has a standard that has been set and a bar they have to reach. When a standard is in place, the wrong men will flee from you because they are not up for the challenge.

Learn to love your Heavenly Father and develop a relationship with Him. Submit your desires to Him and let Him do the rest.

Questions to Journal

Describe the relationship you had with your father as a child.

_____

_____

_____

_____

_____

_____

_____

How has that relationship impacted you as an adult?

_____

_____

_____

_____

_____

_____

_____

Day 31

Do You Love You?

Psalm 46:5

God is within her, she will not fall.[1]

Self-love is a hot topic today. Many people are talking about it, preaching about it, and reading about it. And because it is such a hot topic, when things go south for us, we often question our love for self – every situation in our lives seems to turn into a barometer to measure self-love. The truth is all of us have some level of love for ourselves, or we would not still be alive. But life happens and hurts occur. And those hurts can and will chip away at our self-love depending on how we interpret them.

Think about the new car that you just purchased. From the minute you saw it you were smitten with it. You wash it weekly keeping both the inside and outside clean. You enjoy driving it and showing it off to your friends. But let's say you have a car accident. The dings and dents you now have cause you to lose a bit of love for the car. You no longer wash it every week but now monthly. Soon, the car needs work, so you get upset because it costs you unplanned money. As you can see, the more issues that pop up the more it can chip away at how we feel about it.

So, it is with us. As hurts occur, they chip away at our self-love and that shows up in every decision we make: the man we date or marry, how we treat the person we date or marry, our behavior in the workplace, the career choices we make, how we spend our money, and more importantly, how we treat others.

Although science has proven that we may be born with a genetic disposition towards being optimistic, we are not born with an understanding of how to develop and maintain self-love. Self-love is not something that just exists for many of us. It requires work to maintain. The challenge comes if we have been abused emotionally, physically, verbally; or bullied; or sexually assaulted. Each of those encounters have the ability to impact how we see and feel about ourselves.

If you want to improve your self-love, treat yourself the way you would treat someone that you loved.

*Compliment and speak kindly to yourself.

*Write a list of all the reasons you have to be grateful and look at it daily.

*Take yourself out on dates.

*Invest in your personal and professional development by taking courses and reading books.

*Spend time alone with yourself getting to know you.

*Surround yourself with positive people that do not intentionally try to harm you or others.

*Get good rest, at least seven hours of sleep.

*Eat well-balanced meals.

*Eliminate any negative thoughts about yourself.

*Minimize alcoholic beverages.

*Visit a therapist regularly and practice self-care.

Questions to Journal

Answer the following questions with a yes or no.
1.Are you sensitive to receiving criticism?

_____

1. Do you sometimes wish you were someone else other than yourself?

   _____

2. Have you been a victim of an emotionally, physically, or verbally abusive relationship?

   _____

3. Do you long for validation that comes in the form or compliments and acknowledgement?

   _____

If you answered yes to any of the above questions you may need to do some self-love work. Begin the process by seeing a therapist.

Day 32

Killing the Mean Girl Spirit

Hebrews 13:1-2
Let brotherly love continue. Do not forget to entertain
strangers, for by so doing some have unwittingly entertained
angels.[1]

Many years ago, a friend invited me to meet for drinks at a
new restaurant downtown. As we were relaxing on the patio
of the restaurant sipping our drinks, a lady walked up, said
hello, and sat down at our table. Unbeknownst to me, the
lady was a friend of my friend that she had invited to join us.

For some reason, I was annoyed by her presence. I suppose
it's because I truly did not want her to be there with us or
maybe I wanted my friend to myself. I looked her over,
glanced at her attire, and out of my mean spirit, decided that I
was not going to be kind to her. For most of the evening, I
completely ignored her. When she asked me questions, I
responded with short answers barely acknowledging her
presence. As we sipped on our drinks, I giggled in my
friend's ear, "why did your lil' friend wear her grandmother's
clothes out for drinks?" My insecurities, immature emotions,
and toxic learned behavior would not allow me to make
space for this woman that wanted nothing more than to have
an enjoyable evening with us.

My family always taught me to be careful around women and
to not trust them. So, for many years, I acted out on that. I
was quick to assume the worst about other women and had
very little trust. Additionally, I had a few bad friendships that
went sour that reinforced my family's teachings.

Eventually though, life happened and I had to depend on the support of good girlfriends to get me through. Those girlfriends not only allowed me to cry on their shoulders, but they were there for me and with me when I was at my lowest points, without judgment and gossip. I realized that not all women are our enemies. Not all women want to steal our man, hurt our feelings, or reject us. There are truly some great women out there that know how to do friendships, but we must be open to giving them the opportunity.

Often, when we meet a new woman, our insecurities show up too causing us to compare ourselves to them. Those insecurities cause us to need to feel as if we are winning more than she is and if we believe we have some lack in an area, that is when the competition begins; the one upping, throwing shade, the inability to celebrate successes, the inability to support and show up, and the tearing down, all of those things come from our mangled emotions and insecurities. We must realize that we are all winners. There is no need to compete when you truly believe in your own value.

Overtime, I began to view women as my sisters with their own stories to share and a gift to bring. Not only has this led to peace, but I now have a squad of women standing with me that truly have my back!

Questions to Journal

Describe any situation where you behaved as a "mean girl"?

_____

_____

_____

_____

_____

_____

_____

_____

Describe a situation where someone has been a "mean girl" towards you?

_____

_____

_____

_____

_____

_____

_____

How did both situations make you feel?

_____

_____

_____

_____

_____

Day 33

Bad Friends

Proverbs 16:28
*A perverse man sows strife, And a whisperer (gossiper)
separates the best of friends.*[1]

Good solid friendships are essential and there are many
amazing women out there that know how to do friendships
well. However, it would be ill of me to not give you fair
warning that there are some of our sisters that struggle with
being a friend. I need you to be aware that there are people
that will enter your life under the guise of a friend, yet will
destroy your peace and wreak havoc in your life. Not
everyone is going to be "good people" and not everyone has
your best interest at heart.

In almost every women's group, sorority, church, and social
group there are three types of women that we meet. I am
going to introduce you to them. See if you have met them
before.

Manipulators – Some women come to various groups having earned many accomplishments and have made great strides in their careers. However, these same women have buried insecurities underneath their accomplishments creating an ego that thrives on special attention. Their insecurities breed within them a dark desire to become the "queen bee" of the group. They want all of the attention, all of the power, all of the praise, and for the group to center around them. In order to do this, they seek to eliminate anyone they feel is competition to them in the group. Once they discover their competition, they will deem them their nemesis and create a plot all on their own to snuff that person out.

They begin this process by taking offense at the smallest of issues that do not equate to a heap of beans with the person they have made their nemesis. Then, they create a group text that starts off very innocent and fun, but it excludes the nemesis. The group text soon turns to gossip as the manipulator becomes obsessed with the nemesis taking everything she does personally. The other ladies suddenly begin to despise the nemesis and before you know it, they have completely isolated the nemesis.

Common characteristics of manipulators is they do not like to be challenged and cannot handle critique. Because of this they never grow to maturity and remain in an arrested development. You will find yourself often walking on eggshells around them trying not to offend them. They hide behind their accomplishments, but during conflict they overreact and lash out. Please beware of the manipulator. Their unhealed emotional wounds cause them to leave a path of destruction. They divide groups and leave many women hurt and filled with regrets.

Drama Queens – These folks come across as innocent but deep down they gain gratification from drama, in fact, they may even be addicted to it. They always have the tea and enjoy gossip but never want to be the center of it. They will seek every opportunity they can to carry the gossip and slander a person, but it begins very innocently with questions such as, "why are you not cool with so-and-so?"

Their friendships are typically built off of a shared common enemy. But these friendships lack substance and rarely last because they are not built on a firm foundation. True friendships are built on love, empathy, and mutual interests.

Get Withs – Every superhero, whether good or bad, has a sidekick and so does the manipulator. "Get Withs" are folks that can easily be manipulated and because of that, they quickly fall prey or will "get with" the plan of the manipulator. They have a deep admiration for the manipulator wishing they were able to take her place. They often have trouble discerning right from wrong. They are non-confrontational and because of that they quickly choose the side of the manipulator. Get Withs can't handle being isolated and want to be in the "in crowd" regardless of how toxic it may be. They are rarely leaders and quickly fall in line with the manipulator soon becoming their cheerleader never challenging them and never questioning their actions. Common characteristics of this person is that they are nice, friendly, and easy going yet deeply insecure.

I want each of us to be aware of each of these types of women to assure that this is not how we are showing up. If you have behaved as any of these women, now is the time to do some healing work because the person that you were mean to could have been a value added sent from God. What if the person you isolated could have been the person that was meant to be your next best friend, or the person that introduces you to someone that change your destiny, or the person that supports you the most. You sabotage yourself when you behave similarly to any of the mentioned women.

I hear many women often say that maintaining friendships with other women is difficult. There is some truth to this because human beings, in general, are difficult. We all have different perspectives, experiences, and back stories that impact the way that we view and interact with the world around us. Relationships require love to build, work to maintain, and empathy to sustain.

Questions to Journal

Describe situations and relationships where you may have behaved as each of the above.

_____

_____

_____

_____

_____

_____

_____

_____

What do you believe caused you to take on those roles?

_____

_____

_____

_____

_____

_____

_____

_____

Girl Squad

Proverbs 17:17
A friend loves at all times, and a brother is born for adversity.[1]

Were you taught how to be a good friend in your family? Were healthy adult friendships modeled before you as a child? God has created us to love and to be in community with each other. This is how we will grow and heal, but often toxic learned behavior and unhealed wounds prevent that. I desired long term friendship, but did not know how to be a friend. So, I had to learn what true friendship looks like. I also had to learn not to cause hurts and it is in the smallest of manners that we can hurt someone that loves us, knowingly and unknowingly.

There is a scene on the reality TV show *"Real Housewives of Atlanta"* where Cynthia presents NeNe Leakes with a friendship contract. The other ladies on the show mocked her for it, but I believe Cynthia was on to something.[14] Granted, it may be a bit overboard to present our friends with a legal document; however, my take away from that moment was that we need to have open dialogue with our friends about our boundaries and needs.

It amazes me how we often expect our friends to read our minds to know how to love us and what offends us. Every single friend in my life knows my love language and know that showing up for me is huge and vice versa. They also know that if I disappoint them, I want them to communicate that to me to give me a fair chance to resolve it. That's how friendships are maintained. Let's look at three key points that help us to maintain strong bonds with our friends in what I refer to as the three P's of friendship:

Protection – You must be willing to protect your friends heart, and that requires being honest but in such a way that you do not fracture your friend. Many of us value being outspoken and brutally honest which is a positive trait when it's not mishandled. There is a difference between being honest and being harmful. If you say your truth in a way that causes harm, then you have wasted time while possibly losing a friendship. If you learn to speak your truth in such a way that it motivates, inspires, and empowers, then you have gained the trust and respect of your friend. I firmly believe that this is a skill that not many of us are not born with however once this skill is mastered you will find that you will become a valued commodity in the lives of many.

Presence – Time is as valuable as jewels, in my opinion. Particularly today, many of us work, travel, and care for our families, therefore time is limited. When you make time out of your schedule to show up and be present for someone, you are showing them that you care, and they are valuable to you. Presence is a powerful gift that we give our friends. So, make sure that you show up for the special events in your friend's life—graduations, bridal showers, baby showers, birthday parties, brunches, and the even the casual girl's night out.

Also, we can be present when our friend wants to share their heart with us. Instead of switching the discussion to a topic we'd prefer to talk about or allowing our mind to wander during the conversation, we should be present for our friends emotionally. Hear them out, empathize with them, and try to understand their perspective

Proactive – Conflict amongst friends is inevitable. But it's how we handle the conflict that matters. Oftentimes during a conflict, or when we feel there is tension between us and our friend, we will not have a conversation with them about it. Yet, we will discuss it with everyone else except that person. Because small conflicts can turn into large break-ups, we need to be proactive in our approach to addressing conflict.

Oh, how I longed for Molly and Issa from the TV show "*Insecure*" to calmly address the tension between the two of them very early on.[2] When we feel something is off or there is tension, we should be swift to run to them and share what we feel, with a spirit of humility. Make your goal to resolve the conflict and win back your friend.

Questions to Journal

Which of the three P's do you have the most trouble demonstrating?

_____
_____
_____
_____
_____
_____
_____
_____

Why?

_____
_____
_____
_____
_____
_____
_____

Let Whoever Think Whatever

---

2 Timothy 2:23-25
But avoid foolish and ignorant disputes, knowing that they generate strife. And a servant of the Lord must not quarrel but be gentle to all, able to teach, patient, in humility correcting those who are in opposition, if God perhaps will grant them repentance, so that they may know the truth.[1]

One of the things my mother does when someone says something that does not quite add up or make sense for her is, "oh, OK." This is her way of removing herself from the conversation. She doesn't acknowledge it or give it a ton of thought.

I have spent so much time arguing and being frustrated with people when they say or do something that does not make sense to me. For example, I once had a colleague that believed that she was my leader and even went as far as to act on that. So, I got in my emotions and decided that at every turn I needed to show her that she was not in fact my leader. This created so much drama and tension and wasted my emotions. It also allowed her to live inside of my emotions because each time I saw an email or note from her, I rolled my eyes and got sour. Everything I read or heard from her, it got filtered through my feelings towards her, so she never really got the benefit of the doubt. I had given this woman full rights and access to my emotions.

I had to realize that she had absolutely no control over my day or life. She didn't sign my paycheck, give input into my performance reviews, or determine if I stayed or go. My name certainly wasn't listed under hers on the org chart. But I was giving her power in my life by reacting to her. So, at that point, I made the decision to no longer engage. I allowed her to continue to believe whatever her mind needed her to believe while I was busy living my life, drama free. When she asked me to do something I simply said, "oh, OK" and did what my job description and supervisors that did have an impact on my day discussed for me to do.

Whatever was inside of her that needed to believe she was my boss was her issue. We have to be careful not to allow other people's issues to become our issues by entertaining them and allowing them to impact our emotions and attitude. Some people suffer from fantasy relationships which can also extend beyond romantic relationships. In fantasy relationships, people create relationships and scenarios in their mind to fill a void. But that's not my problem. That's for them to sort out. We can't fix people regardless of how hard we try. But we can control our reactions and how we view it.

But there is another part to all of this: when faced with situations such as this, we must ask ourselves why are we reacting to it. Sometimes, we react and behave defensively when someone does something that pokes or triggers our unhealed emotional wounds. In this instance, this woman was triggering my disdain for overbearing women that I believed sought to control me. You see, I was raised by alpha women that ruled with iron fists. So, I react when anyone tries to be too controlling or wield a certain level of power over me – I'm still healing from my mommy wounds y'all. Pay close attention to your triggers as they are pointing you to wounds that need to be healed.

Questions to Journal

Do you find it difficult to walk away from useless
arguments or conflict?

_____

_____

_____

_____

_____

_____

_____

Why?

_____

_____

_____

_____

_____

_____

What triggers prevent you from walking away from
arguments?

_____

_____

_____

_____

_____

_____

Day 36

Submission

Ephesians 5:21-33
Submit to one another out of reverence for Christ. Wives, submit yourselves to your own husbands as you do to the Lord. For the husband is the head of the wife as Christ is the head of the church, his body, of which he is the Savior. Now as the church submits to Christ, so also wives should submit to their husbands in everything. Husbands, love your wives, just as Christ loved the church and gave himself up for her.[1]

Ladies let's talk about submission. I can remember vividly the day that I bumped into the word submission. I was very new to being a Christian and had joined a women's small group Bible study at my church. We were discussing Ephesians 5:22. The words in this passage of scripture left me confused because this was a foreign principle to me. There weren't any women in my family that were anything similar to what sounded to me like a submissive woman. Therefore, I struggled with this term and the idea behind it for quite some time.

Have you watched the documentary "*Surviving R Kelly?*" Yeah, we all did, right? During this documentary, the singer Sparkle, R. Kelly's protégé mentioned that she was sitting in R. Kelly's living room when she heard a woman, who she believed to be one of his girlfriends, sheepishly ask him for food because she was hungry.[3] That is the image of submission that I had and I knew that was not for me.

But here is what I have learned. Submission is not about asking your husband's permission every time you want to breathe or take a pee. If you marry the right man, a man with a life centered around godly principles, he knows your background and how you are wired. For me, I was raised by alpha women that made the household decisions. Secondly, before I got married, I had my own apartment, a career, and car. My husband knew it would cause chaos and stress to our marriage if he required me to seek his guidance on everything. Furthermore, I honestly don't believe he wanted that type of wife.

Submission begins with agreement. In our marriage, we make our goals together because you can't expect someone to submit to something they have not been bought into or haven't had a voice in. For example, we make our financial goals together. Let's say we make a goal to save money to purchase a home and shortly after, I decide I want to purchase a new car. That's something that I need to discuss with my husband because we, collectively, created a goal to purchase a home together. If he doesn't agree that I should buy the car then I back off – yes, even though it's partially my money – because it's going against what we planned and agreed upon. You see, the goal of submission is to maintain peace and unity. Drama comes when both parties are doing what they want to do.

Secondly, I trust my husband with my whole heart. I would not have married him if I couldn't trust him in that way. So, if he doesn't agree to something, it's off the table because I know and have seen that he has my best interests at heart.

Let us not forget that the Bible says *submit to one another out of reverence for Christ.*[1] For some reason, men tend to conveniently forget that part. Because women tend to be a bit more intuitive, and we can foresee danger due to our emotional capacity, it is in the best interest of our husbands to strongly consider our voices. Harmony in marriage comes when both parties seek the consent of each other prior to making major decisions. Not only does it demonstrate submission on both parts, but mutual respect as well.

Questions to Journal

How can you use this definition of submission to submit to your spouse, manager, etc.?

_____

_____

_____

_____

_____

_____

_____

_____

Day 37

I Am Emotional

Colossians 3:15
And let the peace of God rule in your hearts, to which also you were called in one body; and be thankful.[1]

On this last day, I want to leave you with some final words. There will be many decisions we have to make daily and most of those decisions will involve or impact our emotions. Always choose peace.

Choosing peace begins with constantly developing a relationship with God and healing your emotional wounds. Read scripture daily, pray, read self-help books, visit a therapist and/or a life coach that can create a wellness plan for you.

Yes, it's true that I am emotional. Ladies, we are all emotional beings and express our emotions more than men — that's how God created us and there is absolutely nothing wrong with that. In fact, it is one of our greatest advantages; our emotions allow us to be better leaders and communicators, it gives us strong intuition, and helps us foster empathy.

However, we must learn to manage those emotions, control our overthinking, and place healing where it's necessary so that we can pass that healing down to future generations. Make healing emotional wounds a key part of the generational wealth that you pass down. Choose healing, choose love, and choose peace.

Questions to Journal

What are three things that you will take away from this devotional to implement in your life moving forward?

_____

_____

_____

_____

_____

_____

_____

_____

How can share this knowledge you have gained with your friends and family members?

_____

_____

_____

_____

_____

_____

_____

Notes

1. *The Holy Bible.* New King James Version. (2000). Cincinnati, OH: Thomas Nelson.
2. Rae, Issa (2016-) *Insecure* HBO Productions.
3. Hampton, D (2019). *Surviving R. Kelly* Burnim-Murray
4. Schenck, Laura PH.D. *What is Wise Mind?* https://www.mindfulnessmuse.com/dialectical-behavior-therapy/what-is-wise-mind
5. BET Staff (25 August 2020) *Republican Speaker Says Cops Are Smart to Target Her Adopted Black Son.* https://www.bet.com/news/national/2020/08/25/a bby-johnson-son-cops-adopted-black-son.html
6. https://medium.com/the-mission/a-practical-hack-to-combat-negative-thoughts-in-2-minutes-or-less-cc3d1bddb3af
7. Prakha, Verma. (2017, Nov). *Destroy Negativity From Your Mind with this Simple Exercise.*
8. Schwartz, Allen, PHD. *Shame and Avoidant Personality.* https://www.mentalhelp.net/blogs/shame-and-avoidant-personality-disorder
9. Diorio, MayAnn Dr. (2020). *Sex and Soul Ties* https://maryanndiorio.com/2020/01/27/sex-and-soul-ties-2
10. D, Whit. (2016, June). *The Celibacy Rules Chronicles: Tales of Single Black Grown Woman.* https://thecelibacyrules.blogspot.com/search?q=stro ke
11. Alie, Netisha. (2017, May). *Sex and Spirits: What Happens Spiritually When You*

http://www.mnialive.com/articles/sex-and-spirits-what-happens-spiritually-when-you-have-sex

12. Dean, Signe. (9 June 2018). *Here's How Long it Really Takes To Break A Habit According to Science.* https://www.sciencealert.com/how-long-it-takes-to-break-a-habit-according-to-science

13. Google.com dictionary/grace

14. *The Real Housewives of Atlanta* Season 3 episode 11 (2010) Bravo Productions